Enjoying Wildlife

a guide to RSPB nature reserves

GW00363062

compiled by
BOB SCOTT

The Royal Society for the Protection of Birds is **the** charity that takes action for wild birds and the environment. It has joined with bird and habitat conservation organisations worldwide to form a global partnership called BirdLife International.

Published by The Royal Society for the Protection of Birds, The Lodge, Sandy, Bedfordshire SG19 2DL.

Great care has been taken throughout this book to ensure accuracy, but the RSPB cannot accept any responsibility for any error that may occur.

Cover photograph: Terry Heathcote
Maps: Hilary Welch
Illustrations: John Busby and Dan Powell
Printing and binding: Watkiss Studios Ltd
Distribution: A&C Black (Publishers) Ltd

ISBN no 0 903138 73 5
Registered charity number 207076

45/548/94

CONTENTS

Woodcock

which ever
way you look at it ...

AT80HD High Definition Observation Telescope with 20-60x variable eyepiece or 32 wide angle eyepiece. This telescope features an extra large 80mm objective lens giving a super sharp image with close focusing to 6m.

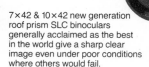

7×42 & 10×42 new generation roof prism SLC binoculars generally acclaimed as the best in the world give a sharp clear image even under poor conditions where others would fail.

8×20B Pocket binoculars are manufactured to the same exacting standards of all Swarovski products. Fitting comfortably into any jacket or breast pocket they are instantly available when needed most.

All fully waterproof.

clearly the best ... SWAROVSKI
OPTIK

For further information on Swarovski products write to:-
SWAROVSKI UK LTD., Fleming Way, Crawley, West Sussex RH10 2NL
Telephone: 0293 525801. Fax: 0293 527346. Telex: 877643 SWARO G

ENJOYING WILDLIFE WITH THE RSPB

When the RSPB bought its first nature reserve at Dungeness in 1931, the staff of the time could not have imagined the magnitude of the change 60 years would bring. The Society now owns, manages or leases over 130 nature reserves throughout the UK, covering over 205,000 acres (83,000 hectares), an area over twice the size of the Isle of Wight.

Reserves are just one part of the RSPB's conservation armoury. They are a means of protecting threatened and vulnerable habitats and species, both birds and other wildlife. Through careful planning, each reserve is managed for the maximum benefit to wildlife, demonstrating what practical conservation management can achieve.

Increasing membership is a clear indication of the growing interest in birds, the countryside and the environment. As people have become more urbanised, so has their desire to visit and enjoy the countryside. RSPB nature reserves provide an excellent opportunity to experience birds and wildlife at first hand in some of the most beautiful parts of the UK. From Cornwall to Shetland; County Fermanagh to Norfolk, the range of habitats and wildlife to be seen is impressive.

I have been lucky enough to visit many of the reserves in the guide and I can assure you of a warm welcome and a fascinating day out. Over one million people visit these special places every year. There is something for everyone, from beginners to experienced birdwatchers alike. I very much hope that you will find *Enjoying Wildlife* a useful introduction to the RSPB's nature reserves and that you will delight in discovering them and their wildlife.

Tony Soper
May 1994

WELCOME TO THE RSPB

RSPB nature reserves provide an excellent opportunity to watch birds and other wildlife. Creating nature reserves is one of the most effective ways of conserving wild birds and the places where they live. The RSPB has been managing land as nature reserves for over 50 years and our knowledge about wild bird conservation is second to none.

Our nature reserves serve two purposes; the conservation of wild birds and their habitats and developing the public's interest and concern for birds and wildlife.

From avocets to eagles

We have many types of reserves, from the ever popular Minsmere on the Suffolk coast, famous for its avocets, to the beautiful, but remote Loch Ruthven in the Scottish Highlands. Many of our reserves offer some facilities for visitors. The most popular have a full range including trails suitable for wheelchairs and pushchairs, tearooms, shops, toilets and interpretative displays and birdwatching hides. Others have more low-key facilities, such as simple trails and hides or perhaps no facilities at all. There will always be some reserves where visitors can enjoy a quiet, natural experience.

Walking at Ynys-hir, learning at Sandwell Valley

There are many ways to enjoy our nature reserves: a walk in the beautiful Welsh countryside at Ynys-hir, learning about wildlife at Sandwell Valley, or taking the family bird-watching at Pulborough Brooks. There are nature reserves to suit all tastes - from a conservation experience for the whole family to those who want to get away from it all. On many reserves there are special events, such as guided walks, children's activities, talks and demonstrations. You can obtain details of these from the reserve or the local tourist information centre.

Saving a place for birds

The birds and wildlife on our reserves must always come first. So on a few reserves it is necessary to restrict visitors to certain areas or even have no visitors at all because of the fragility of the habitat and wildlife.

This guide aims to help you enjoy the birds and wildlife on our nature reserves. We hope that you will enjoy using it and, more importantly, enjoy visiting many of our nature reserves.

Barbara S Young

Barbara Young
Chief Executive

WHAT WE DO

The RSPB believes that the beauty of birds and nature enriches the lives of many people but also that nature conservation is fundamental to a healthy environment on which the survival of the human race depends. The RSPB therefore strives for the conservation of wild birds and the environment on which they depend, primarily in the UK but increasingly in Europe and elsewhere in the world.

The RSPB is Europe's largest wildlife conservation charity with over 860,000 members. The RSPB has joined with bird and habitat conservation organisations worldwide to form a global partnership called BirdLife International.

In addition to our UK headquarters in Bedfordshire and Scottish headquarters in Edinburgh, we have a network of country and regional offices throughout the UK. The RSPB is a major force in wildlife conservation and adopts a realistic and professional approach to its work. We seek to safeguard our natural heritage by:

- promoting the conservation of wild birds and their habitats.
- research into conservation issues and formulation of policies and proposals.
- working with government to create solutions to the problems.
- working with industry, landowners and the public to provide a better future for wildlife and the environment.
- buying and managing land as nature reserves.
- placing strong emphasis on youth and education.

Some facts about the RSPB

- We are supported by over 860,000 members including 130,000 members of the YOC.
- We have over 170 members' groups, who raise funds and public awareness of our activities.
- We benefit from 20,000 days of voluntary work each year.
- We are leaders in bird conservation research, both in the UK and abroad.
- We are involved in conservation projects in over 20 countries worldwide.
- Our award winning members' magazine *Birds*, is read by 1.8 million people.
- We provide education advice to about 37,000 schools and higher education colleges.

Our nature reserves

- We own or lease over 130 reserves throughout the UK.
- Our land holding totals over 83,000 hectares (205,000 acres) which is over twice the size of the Isle of Wight.
- More than 1,000,000 people visit our reserves each year.
- Over 50,000 children come to our reserves on educational visits each year.

Osprey

A partnership for wildlife

Since 1989, the RSPB and *Barclays Bank* have developed a close partnership for nature conservation. The Bank has been integral to many RSPB projects, enabling us to extend and enhance our nature reserves throughout the UK. With *Barclays'* help we have purchased land, planted woodlands, maintained reedbeds for bitterns and installed dams and sluices to revitalise wet meadows. We look forward to our continuing partnership with *Barclays,* so that together we can ensure future generations will be able to enjoy a countryside rich in wildlife.

VISITING RSPB NATURE RESERVES

Visitors are welcome at all nature reserves listed in this guide. For each reserve we list the facilities available. At some, such as Pulborough Brooks and Leighton Moss, we offer tearooms, car parks and shops. However, we do not provide a full range of facilities on all of our nature reserves. This is either because the habitat is not suitable for large numbers of visitors or financial factors.

On all our nature reserves, the interests of wildlife must come first. With this in mind we ask visitors to help us by considering the following:

Access
On many reserves certain areas will be open to the public, the remainder being kept quiet for wildlife. To avoid unnecessary disturbance, please keep to the marked trails and paths.

Opening times
Visitor and information centres, hides, car parks and toilets on some nature reserves are not necessarily open all the hours the reserve is.

Entry charges
On some reserves there are entry charges for non-RSPB members. These reserves are clearly marked in the guide. RSPB and YOC members are admitted free of charge. If you are a member remember to take your membership card with you. Where additional services are provided, eg escorted walks and boat trips, additional charges for both members and non-members are sometimes levied.

Group visits
Where possible the warden or another member of staff will be happy to escort groups around our reserves. Any group of over 15 planning a visit should contact the warden to make suitable arrangements.

Dogs
To prevent unnecessary disturbance to wildlife, we regret that dogs are not welcome on RSPB nature reserves (guide dogs excepted).

Schools

The RSPB offers a comprehensive service for schools on many nature reserves. The education programmes are designed to complement the relevant national curricula. The programmes are run by trained RSPB teacher naturalists and the emphasis is on a hands-on approach to environmental education. The following reserves offer education programmes; for further details please contact the relevant reserve or RSPB office.

Arne

Aylesbeare Common

Bempton Cliffs

Coombes Valley

Dungeness

Eastwood

Fairburn Ings

Hodbarrow

Fowlmere

Leighton Moss

Minsmere

Nagshead

Pulborough Brooks

**Radipole Lake
and Lodmoor**

Rye House Marsh

Sandwell Valley

Stour Wood

Strumpshaw Fen

Titchwell Marsh

Portmore Lough

Baron's Haugh

Loch of Kinnordy

Loch of Strathbeg

Lochwinnoch

Vane Farm

Cwm Clydach

Lake Vyrnwy

South Stack Cliffs

Ynys-hir

PRACTICAL ADVICE FOR VISITORS

Can I visit by public transport?

For those who want to use public transport to visit our nature reserves, the nearest railway station is given. In most cases, a bus or taxi will be needed to complete the journey to the reserve.

What should I wear?

Even in the summer be prepared for a sudden change in the weather, particularly on exposed and upland reserves. Carry warm and waterproof clothes just in case. On some reserves the paths may be uneven and rugged so stout footwear should be worn. Wellington boots are recommended for wetland reserves.

Are children welcome on RSPB nature reserves?

Yes! All members of the family can find something of interest on our reserves. Those with visitor centres are particularly suitable for families. Some paths on reserves may be unsuitable for pushchairs and young children may need to be carried.

Are the reserves accessible to visitors with special needs?

There are facilities suitable for visitors with special needs on many of our nature reserves. Access for disabled people is being constantly upgraded. In many instances, hides have been adapted for wheelchair access and special paths and board walks have been installed. A free leaflet with more details is available from RSPB headquarters at The Lodge.

Will there be someone to answer my questions?

Where possible on our most visited reserves a warden or volunteer will be pleased to answer any queries you may have. However, on some of our less visited reserves a member of staff or volunteer may not be available.

How do I explore the reserve?

On most nature reserves there are specially laid out nature trails and waymarked paths. Some reserves have trail leaflets, while on others there may be path-side display boards. To avoid disturbing wildlife we ask you to keep to the paths.

Can I get something to eat and drink?

Where appropriate we are introducing some refreshment facilities on some nature reserves. Some, such as Pulborough Brooks and Leighton Moss, have a tearoom where you can get a light meal or snack; others such as Titchwell Marsh have more limited facilities, such as vending machines. On some reserves it is not possible to provide refreshments, but picnic tables are often available.

What birds can I expect to see?

For each reserve we give you an idea of the birds you might expect to see and the time of year that they are there. Because of their very nature, we cannot guarantee that you will see any or all of the birds listed.

Is there anything else to see on an RSPB nature reserve?

Yes. Lots of other wildlife, from mammals to insects, from fungi to flowers can be found on our nature reserves. For each reserve, we give a brief description of what other wildlife you might see.

Are there events and guided walks?

Many of our nature reserves have programmes of events throughout the year, including guided walks, bat evenings, dawn chorus walks and talks. For more information on these events contact the reserve direct.

Can I help on an RSPB nature reserve?

We always welcome volunteers to work on our nature reserves. You may want to do practical management work or you may be happier helping in one of the shops. If you would like further information on how you can help, please contact our Reserves Management Department at The Lodge.

If you do not want to work on a reserve, but would like to help us there are many other things you can do, from helping at one of our offices to joining one of over 170 local members' groups. For more information please contact: The Youth and Volunteer unit at the Lodge.

On all of our nature reserves we have to undertake some management work. This is done to improve the habitat for wildlife and to improve the visitor facilities. Where possible we try to avoid disturbing visitors while this work is in progress.

While we expect the arrangements given in this guide to be accurate we maintain the right to modify them if necessary.

HOW TO USE THIS GUIDE

The reserves are listed alphabetically by RSPB region.

 Look for the sign! Special brown RSPB signs are being introduced throughout the country to guide visitors to our major reserves.

 The extent of the reserve is shown by the shaded area on the maps. In some cases it is not possible to show the whole area.

 The reserve entrance is shown on the map and written directions are also given. An Ordnance Survey map reference is also provided.

P Where a car park at or near the reserve is provided this is shown. Where informal or limited parking is available, the words 'car parking' are used.

£ On some reserves there is an entrance charge for non-RSPB members. This charge is refunded if you join the RSPB on the day of your visit.

WC Toilets are available on or beside the reserve. *Special note:* where possible on our major reserves we do try to provide toilet facilities. However, it is not always possible to do so.

IC Many reserves have some form of information centre. These may range from purpose built visitors' centres with teaching facilities, shops and toilets to more low-key outdoor interpretative displays. The centres may not always be open all the hours that the reserve is.

 Reserve suitable for visitors with special needs.

G Illustrated leaflets and booklets are available for many of our nature reserves. They are on sale at the reserve or by post from The Lodge.

S A number of nature reserves have RSPB shops selling an extensive range of goods from binoculars and books to bird food and feeders.

S Main shop   **S** Small retail outlet

Tearoom with a full range of hot and cold drinks, snacks and light meals.

Drinks and light snacks available.

i Local Tourist Information Centres will be able to provide information on accommodation and other attractions in the area. You may also find information on accommodation in the Classified section of *Birds* magazine and the advertisements in this guide. However, inclusion in this guide or *Birds* magazine does not imply any endorsement by the RSPB.

New telephone codes

Please note that from 16 April 1995 you will need to add a 1 to all telephone codes shown in this guide. For example, the phone number for the RSPB headquarters will change from 0767 680551 to 01767 680551.

Map of RSPB nature reserves by RSPB region

C – Central
EA – East Anglia
ES – East Scotland
NE – North of England
NI – Northern Ireland
NS – North Scotland
NW – North-West
SE – South-East
SW – South-West
SWS – South and West Scotland
WA – Wales

Balranald

Fairy
NS

Glenborrodale
Coll
Killie

Loch Gruinart

Rathlin Island Cliffs
Lough Foyle
Wood of Cree

Castlecaldwell

NI

Carlingford
Lough Islands

Sout
and

Mawddach Vall

Ramsey Island
Grassholm

Chapel Woo

Aylesbeare

Hayle Estuary
Marazion Marsh

oup Cliffs
k Head
Loons
n Hoy

North Hill
rumland
Mill Dam
Birsay Moor
Hobbister
Copinsay

Lumbister
Fetlar
Loch of Spiggie

Culbin Sands
Udale Bay
Loch Ruthven
Loch of Strathbeg
Loch Garten (Abernethy)
nsh Marshes
ES
Fowlsheugh
Loch of Kinnordy
aid
Vane Farm
arons' Haugh
och
WS
Ken-Dee Marshes
Campfield Marsh
alloway
Haweswater
St Bees Head
ow
Leighton Moss & Morecambe Bay
Bempton Cliffs
NE
Fairburn Ings
NW
Blacktoft Sands
Eastwood
Tetney Marshes
Dee Estuary
Cliffs
kes
Coombes Valley and Churnet Valley Woods
Titchwell Marsh
Lake Vyrnwy
Frampton Marshes
ys-hir
Sandwell Valley
Snettisham
Strumpshaw/Surlingham
Dyffryn Wood
Nene Washes
Berney Marshes/ Breydon Water
Wye/Elan
C
Ouse Washes
EA
Minsmere
Dinas/Gwenffrwd
Highnam Woods
The Lodge
Wolves Wood
North Warren
Havergate Island
n Clydach
Nagshead
Fowlmere
Boyton Marshes
Stour Estuary
Rye House Marsh
Old Hall Marshes
SW
Church Wood
Northward Hill
Nor Marsh/Motney
Elmley Marshes
West Sedgemoor
Pulborough Brooks
SE
Tudeley Woods
Blean Woods
Garston Wood
Langstone
Fore Wood
Dungeness
Exe Estuary
Arne
Harbour
Adur Estuary
Radipole Lake & Lodmoor
Pilsey Island

HOW TO SEE MORE BIRDS

Seeing birds is partly a matter of experience, knowing when and where to look, and partly commonsense. Being quiet, careful and inconspicuous is a helpful start. People visiting nature reserves, excitedly anticipating what they may see, are often still talking as they reach the first hide. 'Have you got the field guide?' 'Did you remember the coffee?' 'Do you think we might see an avocet? Oh, this tripod is a nuisance'. By then, birds along the early part of the trail have sunk out of sight, those near the hide have been warned that people are approaching - and people already in the hide are annoyed that the birds they were watching so closely have now moved away.

It is far better to be organised before leaving the reserve centre and to start quietly and ready to see birds right away. Look about you as you walk - upwards and back where you have come from as well as from side to side - and be alert to the slightest sound. No-one needs to wear full camouflage to take a walk around an RSPB reserve, but sober colours help. More important, though, are quiet, careful movements. Even stopping to look at a bird is a skill that can be improved: jerk to a stop mid-stride, with a lightning lift of the binoculars (and a loudly-hissed 'Look at that!') and the bird is guaranteed to fly off. Stop more gently if you can! It is sudden change that scares birds more than smooth movement.

Make use of cover, such as banks, hedges and bushes. If you can, sit still and let birds come to you, especially in a woodland clearing or at a suitable spot overlooking a pool. Take note of features ahead, so you are ready to look each way along a ride or a stream that you cross - many birds like the edges of such features but you need to be ready for them.

Keep below the tops of open banks where you will be silhouetted against the sky, especially at reserves with wildfowl and waders. If a bird dives into a bush, back away, sit down and wait. In a hide, try not to bump equipment against the boards, or to bang the shutters. Keep your hands inside the shutters and be patient. When the birds don't know you are there, you see them at their best, relaxed and undisturbed.

Rob Hume, Editor *Birds* magazine

How to join the RSPB

Thanks to the loyal support of over 860,000 members, the RSPB, the largest wildlife conservation charity in Europe, is able to make an effective contribution to the conservation of our wild birds and the places where they live. To continue and expand this important work, we need even more support. You can help us by joining the RSPB today.

In return you will:

- have free admission to over 100 of our nature reserves

- receive our superb, full-colour magazine *Birds*, free, four times a year (or *Bird Life* six times a year for young people)

- be eligible to join the countrywide network of members' groups

Please see overleaf for the joining form. The completed form should be sent to: RSPB, Freepost, The Lodge, Sandy, Bedfordshire SG19 2BR.

For more information about membership of the RSPB, the various additional categories of membership or if you wish to join over the telephone using your credit card, please ring the RSPB headquarters on 01767 680551.

I/We would like to join the RSPB/YOC as indicated below:

☐ RSPB single £20

☐ YOC single £7

☐ YOC joint £9 (for all children at one address)

Annual subscription rates shown. If membership is a gift, please supply your name and address separately.
BLOCK CAPITALS PLEASE

Title ☐   Initials ☐   Surname ☐

Address ☐
☐
☐

Postcode ☐

Names of children (for YOC membership)   Date of birth

☐ ☐

☐ ☐

☐ ☐

☐ ☐

I enclose a cheque/PO (pay RSPB) or debit my Access/Visa card no:

☐☐☐☐☐☐☐☐☐☐☐☐☐☐☐☐

Expiry date ☐   For amount £ ☐

Cardholder's signature

☐

(Please state cardholder's address if different from above.)

Send to **RSPB, Freepost,**
The Lodge, Sandy, Bedfordshire SG19 2BR.
Photocopies of this form are acceptable.

Code P5526

England

Barn owl

ARNE,
DORSET

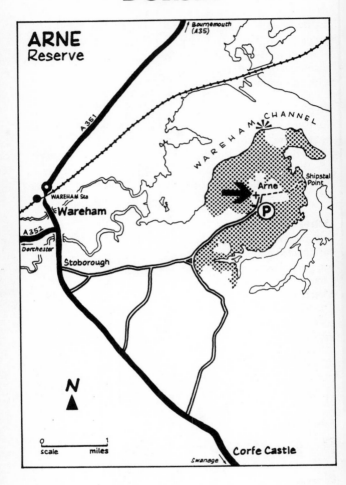

Location

The Arne peninsula lies in Poole Harbour east of Wareham, and the reserve is approached off the A351 road to Swanage, 1/2 mile (1 km) from Wareham, turning as signposted in Stoborough. SY/473882. The nearest railway station is at Wareham (4 miles - 6.4 km).

Arne reserve is one of the last remaining areas of Dorset heathland. The reserve can be enjoyed from a number of paths, one of which leads to the beach. There are birdwatching hides overlooking the estuary.

Habitat

An extensive heathland covering 1,258 acres (524 ha) of heather, gorse and scattered pines with some valley bogs. Also mixed woodland, fens with reedbeds and creeks with saltmarsh on the edge of Poole Harbour.

Birds

Dartford warblers, nightjars and stonechats breed on the heaths, and sparrowhawks and woodpeckers in the woods. Large flocks of black-tailed godwits and spotted redshanks use the foreshore during migration. Wintering birds include red-breasted mergansers, goldeneyes, wigeons and hen harriers.

Other wildlife

Roe and sika deer, all six species of British reptiles including sand lizard and smooth snake, and 22 species of dragonflies are part of Arne's rich animal life.

Visiting

The Shipstal part of the reserve is open at all times, but the rest of the reserve is closed except to parties by prior arrangement with the warden. The reserve car park, with toilets, is in Arne village and the public bridleway to Shipstal, with its nature trail and leaflet, starts opposite the church. Please keep to the paths and trackways, except on the beach.

Facilities

P £ (car park) **WC G s**

Warden

Bryan Pickess, Syldata, Arne, Wareham BH20 5BJ.

i The Whitehouse, Shore Road, Swanage BH19 1LB (tel: 0929 422885).

AYLESBEARE COMMON,
DEVON

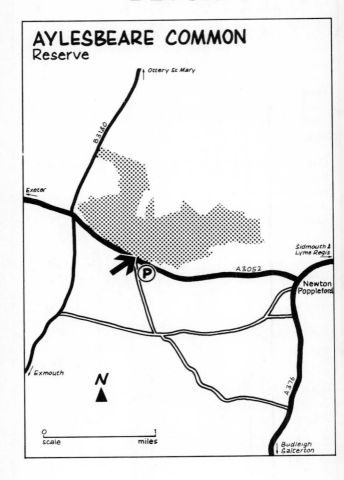

Location

Comprising part of the Pebblebed Commons of south Devon, the reserve lies to the north of the A3052 Lyme Regis to Exeter road one mile (1.6 km) west of Newton Poppleford. SY/057898. The nearest railway station is in Exeter (6 miles - 9.6 km).

Aylesbeare Common is a quiet heathland reserve with a number of footpaths and a waymarked trail. The East Devon Way crosses the reserve.

Habitat
Covering 527 acres (220 ha) the reserve has both dry and wet heathland with valley bogs, some woodland and willow scrub.

Birds
Dartford warblers, nightjars, stonechats, yellowhammers, tree pipits and grasshopper warblers breed on the heath, and marsh tits and wood warblers in the woodland.

Other wildlife
Plants include dwarf gorse, pale butterwort, bog pimpernel and royal fern. Roe deer, wood cricket, adder and up to 23 dragonfly species occur. Thirty-eight species of butterfly have been recorded.

Visiting
The reserve is open at all times, but please keep to the footpaths and firebreak paths from which there are good views of the reserve. A waymarked trail starts opposite the public car park.

Facilities
P

Warden
Pete Gotham, Valley Barn, Hawkerland, Colaton Raleigh, Sidmouth, Devon EX10 0JA.

i The Old Town Hall, The Flexton, Ottery St Mary, Devon EX11 1DJ (tel: 0404 813964).

CHAPEL WOOD, DEVON

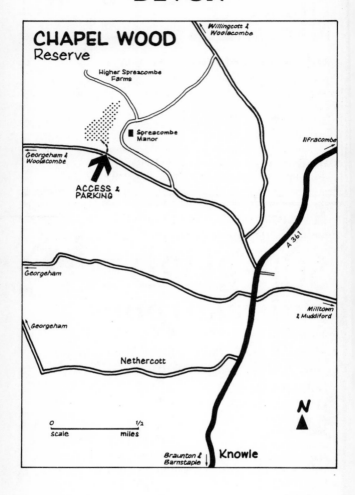

Location

Situated near the north Devon coast, this reserve is approached from the A361 Barnstaple to Ilfracombe road, turning to Spreacombe two miles (3 km) north of Braunton. SS/483413. The nearest railway station is in Barnstaple (10 miles - 16 km).

This small 14 acre (6 ha) woodland reserve can be visited by contacting the honorary warden. There are a number of paths through the wood.

Habitat
A valley woodland of oak, beech and birch.

Birds
Nuthatches, treecreepers, redstarts, marsh tits, pied and spotted flycatchers, all three species of woodpecker and occasionally ravens and buzzards nest on or near the reserve. Woodcocks, redwings and fieldfares occur in winter; dippers are present all year.

Other wildlife
Foxes, red deer and badgers sometimes visit the wood.

Visiting
To visit the reserve please write to the honorary warden, enclosing an SAE. Cars should be parked on the verge near the entrance stile from which visitors cross a field to the reserve gate with the RSPB sign. A path, with several branches, encircles the wood.

Honorary warden
Cyril Manning, 8 Chicester Park, Woolacombe, North Devon EX34 7BZ.

i North Devon Library, Tully Street, Barnstaple, Devon EX31 1TY (tel: 0271 388583).

Green woodpecker

EXE ESTUARY RESERVES,
DEVON

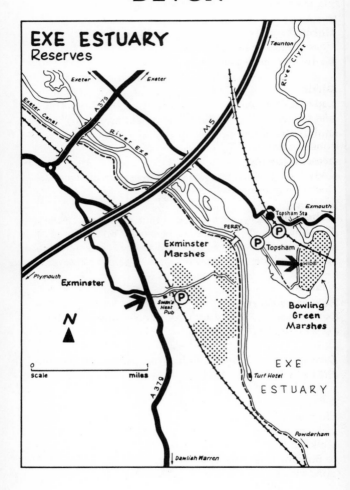

Location

The two reserves lie at the head of the Exe Estuary, on opposite sides of the river. Exminster Marshes can be approached from the A379 Exeter to Dawlish road, close to Exminster village. Bowling Green Marsh lies between the estuaries of the Rivers Exe and Clyst, just south-east of the village of Topsham where there is a railway station.

These two wetland reserves lie alongside the Exe Estuary south of Exeter. A hide overlooks Bowling Green Marsh while canal towpaths provide excellent views over marshes at Exminster.

Habitat
Coastal grazing marshes covering 238 acres (96 ha) with freshwater ditches and shallow floods.

Birds
Lapwings and redshanks breed in the meadows at Exminster, and sedge, reed and Cetti's warblers along the canal banks and ditch edges. Both reserves attract large numbers of roosting and feeding estuary birds. These include: brent geese, wigeons, golden plovers, lapwings, black-tailed godwits, curlews, whimbrels and redshanks; there is a flock of wintering avocets nearby.

Other wildlife
The ditches have many plants, including frogbit, flowering rush and water chickweed. Seventeen species of dragonflies and damselflies have been recorded.

Visiting
Exminster Marshes: Access at all times. The visitor car park is just over the railway bridge beyond the Swan's Nest public house, at SX/954872. Pedestrian access is usually possible to/from Topsham via the foot ferry. There are excellent views of the reserve from Swan's Nest Lane, and the canal bank tow-paths, and of the estuary from the footpath from Turf Hotel to Powderham church.
Bowling Green Marsh: Access at all times. Park at either Holman Way car park SX/968881 (close to Topsham railway station), or The Quay car park at SX/966879, and walk via The Strand and the Goatwalk (alongside the river) to Bowling Green Lane. A hide along this lane provides good views of the marsh.

Facilities

Warden
Malcolm Davies, c/o RSPB South-West England Office (page 295).

i Civic Centre, Paris Street, Exeter EC1 1JJ (tel: 0392 265700).

GARSTON WOOD,
DORSET

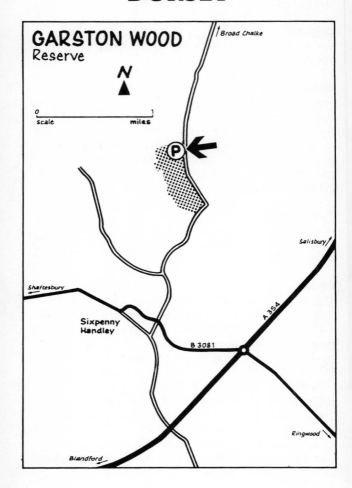

Location

Situated on the chalk downs of Cranborne Chase, the reserve is approached from the main Salisbury-Blandford Road one mile north of Sixpenny Handley on the road to Broad Chalke. SU/004194. The nearest railway station is in Salisbury (15 miles - 24 km).

This small coppiced ancient woodland reserve offers pleasant walks on a number of paths. It is at its best when the bluebells and wood anemones are in flower during May.

Habitat
An ancient coppice of hazel, field maple and ash with oaks covering 84 acres (34 ha).

Birds
Nightingales, turtle doves, garden warblers and yellowhammers nest in the young coppice while marsh tits, nuthatches, great spotted woodpeckers and tawny owls favour the mature woodland. Woodcocks and bramblings occur in winter.

Other wildlife
The magnificent spring flowers include the unusual toothwort, Solomon's seal and both bird's-nest and greater butterfly orchids. White admiral and silver-washed fritillary butterflies may be seen along the rides. Roe deer, badger and dormouse are present.

Visiting
Access at all times from the small car park along the woodland paths.

Facilities
P

Warden
Occasionally present: c/o Arne Reserve (see page 25).

i Marsh and Ham Car Park, West Street, Blandford DT11 7AW (tel: 0258 454770).

HAYLE ESTUARY,
CORNWALL

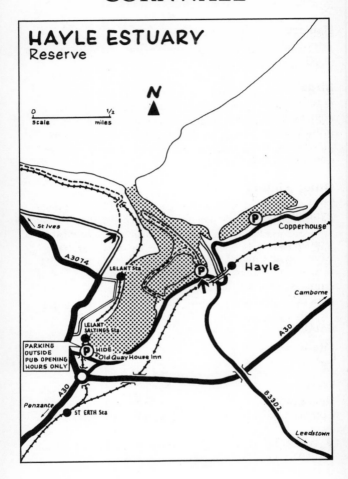

Location

Situated in the town of Hayle but the best vantage point is from the Old Quay House Inn car park as you leave Hayle towards St Ives. SW/546364. The nearest railway station is in the town of Hayle.

This reserve offers excellent opportunities to watch estuary wildlife at close quarters, particularly in the autumn and winter. There is one hide at the south-west end of the reserve in the grounds of the Old Key House Inn.

Habitat
Intertidal mudflats, saltmarsh, sand dunes and beach covering 356 acres (144 ha).

Birds
A refuge for wildfowl and waders in severe winters: wigeons, teals, shelducks, lapwings, grey and golden plovers and curlews all visit the reserve. Peregrines are regular. Great northern divers and ring-billed gulls winter. The reserve is renowned for its rarities especially in autumn.

Other wildlife
Over 225 species of plants have been recorded, including pyramidal and southern marsh orchid in the sand dunes.

Visiting
Access at all times. There is a small hide at the Old Quay House where there is limited parking (12 noon - 2 pm only - unless using the Inn). There is a small charge for the car park at Copperhouse in Commercial Road.

Facilities

Warden
Dave Flumm, 6 Beacon Crescent, Sancreed, Penzance, Cornwall TR20 8QR.

i Tourist Information Centre, Station Road, Penzance TR18 2NF (tel: 0736 62207).

LODMOOR,
DORSET

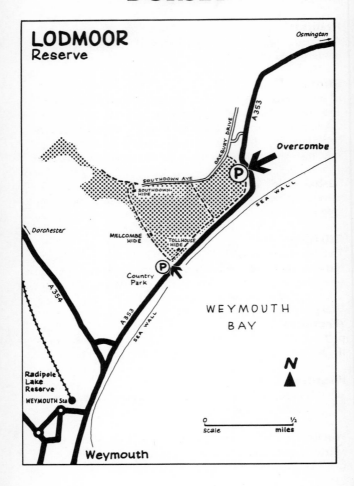

Location

Situated behind the beach and seawall on the east side of
Weymouth, the reserve is entered from opposite either the
Preston Beach Road or Overcombe Corner car parks off
the A353 road to Wareham. The nearest railway station is
in Weymouth (1 mile - 1.6 km).

Lodmoor Reserve is to the north-east of Weymouth next to the sea. The paths are suitable for wheelchairs and pushchairs. There are three hides overlooking the marsh and reedbeds.

Habitat
A grazing marsh of 165 acres (66 ha) with dykes, shallow pools, reedbeds and scrub.

Birds
In summer, the reedbeds and scrub contain reed, sedge and grasshopper warblers, bearded tits, reed buntings and Cetti's warblers; while mallards, teals, shovelers, shelducks and yellow wagtails breed on the moor. Hundreds of swallows, martins and yellow wagtails occur on migration; a variety of waders, such as greenshank and green sandpiper, use the pools to feed. In winter, mallards, teals, shovelers, gadwalls and wigeons use the reserve. Large numbers of lapwings can also be found on the moor in winter.

Other wildlife
The large black and yellow spider *Argiope bruennichi* is found in the grassy banks. Roe deer can sometimes be seen in the reedbeds.

Visiting
Access at all times from either public car parks to a perimeter path which, via Oakbury Drive and Southdown Avenue, links three hides overlooking the moor.

Facilities
P   WC   ♿

Warden
Martin Slater, Radipole Lake Nature Centre, The Swannery Car Park, Weymouth, Dorset DT4 7TZ.

i RSPB Radipole Lake Centre, The Swannery Car Park, Weymouth (tel: 0305 778313) or Weymouth Tourist Information Centre, The King's Statue, The Esplanade, Weymouth DT4 7AN (tel: 0305 365221).

MARAZION MARSH, CORNWALL

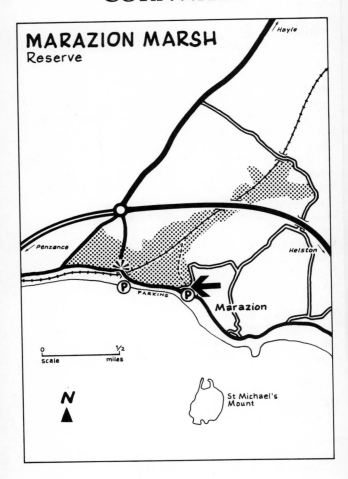

Location

Situated on the seafront road between Penzance and
Marazion. Turn off the A30 from Hayle towards St Michael's
Mount, Marazion, passing over the railway which bisects
the reserve. The nearest railway station is in Penzance
(2.5 miles - 4 km).

This is a small wetland reserve overlooking St Michael's Mount. A public footpath goes through the site following the Red River to a footbridge leading to a small hide next to the water.

Habitat
A marsh with shallow pools, reeds and scrub covering 131 acres (53 ha).

Birds
Breeding reed, sedge and Cetti's warblers, reed buntings, grey herons, mallards, coots and moorhens. The marsh is famous for its migrant aquatic warblers and waders in August and September.

Other wildlife
On the reserve 350 species of plants have been recorded and 318 insects including 19 dragonfly and 22 butterfly species.

Visiting
Access at all times. There are no facilities, but visitors may enter at the eastern end of the reserve from the charity car park at Green Lane where a public footpath borders the Red River. There is no wheelchair access at present. Toilets are on the seafront.

Warden
Dave Flumm, 6 Beacon Crescent, Sancreed, Penzance, Cornwall TR20 8QR.

i Tourist Information Centre, Station Road, Penzance TR18 2NF (tel: 0736 62207).

Sedge warbler

RADIPOLE LAKE, DORSET

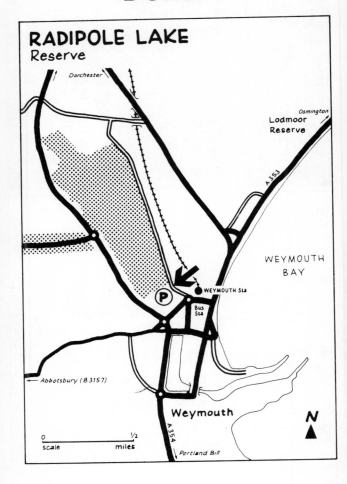

Location

Situated within the town of Weymouth, the reserve entrance and visitor centre are located at the Swannery Car Park close to the seafront and railway station and are well signposted. SY/677796. The nearest railway station is in Weymouth (430 yards - 400 m).

A popular nature reserve with birdwatchers and families alike, it offers firm paths, birdwatching hides and a visitor centre. An exciting programme of events is carried out throughout the year.

Habitat
Reedbeds with large and small shallow pools, rough pasture and scrub covering 222 acres (90 ha).

Birds
Reed, sedge and grasshopper warblers, mute swans, gadwalls, teals and great crested grebes all breed. Grey herons, cormorants and sparrowhawks are regularly seen throughout the year while wigeons, tufted ducks and pochards, water pipits and large numbers of water rails are among the winter visitors. Other birds include the rare Cetti's warbler and bearded tit.

Other wildlife
Mammals include roe deer, fox and a variety of bats. A wide variety of butterflies, moths and dragonflies is recorded including no less than seven rare moths.

Visiting
Open access to most parts of the reserve. There is a charge to enter the northern section of the reserve. Firm paths lead to three hides with wheelchair access. Hides are open 8 am to dusk. The centre and shop are open daily all year from 9 am - 5 pm. Public toilets are available in the adjacent car park. This is currently a 'long-stay' car park where RSPB members can take advantage of a reduced charge.

Facilities
P £ WC IC ♿ G S

Warden
Martin Slater, Radipole Lake Nature Centre, The Swannery Car Park, Weymouth, Dorset DT4 7TZ.

i Tourist Information Centre, King's Statue, The Esplanade, Weymouth DT4 7AN (tel: 0305 765221).

WEST SEDGEMOOR,
SOMERSET

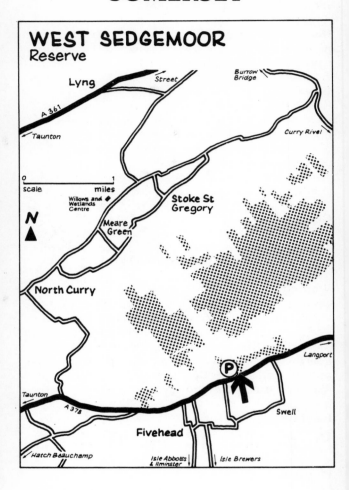

Location

Forming part of the Somerset Levels, this reserve is signposted off the A378 road from Taunton to Langport one mile (1.6 km) east of Fivehead village. ST/361238. The nearest railway station is in Taunton (10 miles - 16 km).

The low-lying wet meadows are ideal for breeding wading birds and wildfowl in the winter. There is a waymarked path, which is suitable for wheelchairs to a viewpoint overlooking the meadows. There are two hides, one in the woodland and the other on the edge of the meadows.

Habitat

Low-lying wet meadows covering 1,300 acres (526 ha) with droves and ditches and bordered by deciduous woodland on the southern scarp. Winter flooding dries in the spring to enable hay-cutting and cattle grazing.

Birds

Redshanks, curlews, snipe, lapwings, black-tailed godwits, yellow wagtails, sedge warblers, whinchats and quails nest on the moor where whimbrels are seen regularly on migration. Large flocks of lapwings are joined in winter by golden plovers, teals, wigeons and Bewick's swans. One of Britain's largest heronries of about 80 pairs is in Swell Wood, where buzzards, blackcaps, marsh tits and nightingales also breed.

Other wildlife

Marsh marigold, ragged robin and marsh orchid flower in the meadows and water violet in the dykes. Roe deer are often seen.

Visiting

Access at all times to the woodland car park, heronry hide and waymarked path with a viewpoint across the moor. There is another hide at the edge of the moor below. The Willows and Wetlands visitors' centre is nearby (see map; tel: 0823 490249).

Facilities

P ♿ **G**

Warden

Les Street, Dewlands Farm, Redhill, Curry Rivel, Langport, Somerset TA10 0PH.

i The Library, Corporation Street, Taunton, Somerset TA1 4AN (tel: 0823 274785).

ADUR ESTUARY,
WEST SUSSEX

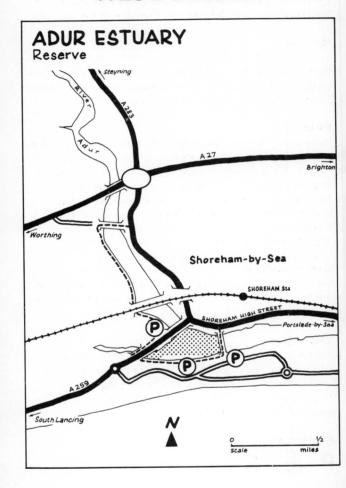

Location

Occupying a portion of the tidal River Adur within Shoreham-by-Sea, the reserve may be viewed from various vantage points from the footbridge and footpath along the south side and from the view point by the Norfolk Bridge. TQ/211050. The nearest railway station is in Shoreham (1/4 mile - 400 m).

A public footpath circles the reserve, giving good views. The reserve is particularly good for watching small wading birds and other waterbirds during the winter.

Habitat
Twenty-five acres (10 ha) of intertidal mudflats and saltmarsh.

Birds
Redshanks, ringed plovers, dunlins and grey plovers feed in winter on the mud, roosting at high tides on the nearby shore or airfield. Curlew sandpipers, bar-tailed godwits, whimbrels and rarer waders are occasionally seen together with cormorants, shelducks and several species of gull including yellow-legged herring gull and Mediterranean gull.

Other wildlife
Sea purslane, glasswort and sea aster are some of the saltwater plants.

Visiting
Good views may be obtained of the river from adjacent footpaths near Shoreham High Street. An illustrated leaflet is available from the RSPB South-East England Office (page 295). There is a car park at the edge of the recreation ground by Norfolk Bridge.

Facilities
P

Warden
Andy Polkey, 46 Stein Road, Southbourne, Emsworth, Hampshire PO10 8LD.

 10 Bartholomew Square, Brighton, East Sussex BN1 1JS (tel: 0652 657053).

Free for Life

GUARANTEED

**Why continue to pay an
annual fee for your credit card?
Switch to our Free for Life RSPB
Visa Credit Card and you'll never have to
pay an annual fee again - GUARANTEED.**

Because it's a Visa Credit Card, you'll be able to use
it at over 10 million outlets worldwide. You can use
it to pay for goods and services anywhere you see
the famous Visa symbol.

**To qualify, you simply have to use the card at least
10 times a year.**

For every successful application, the RSPB receives
£5 from The Co-operative Bank. Furthermore, every
time you use the card, the Society receives 2.5p for
every £10 spent. All this at no extra cost to yourself.

To find out more about this remarkable offer simply
ask the reserves staff or phone us on 0767 680551,
between 9 am and 5.15 pm Monday to Friday.

Remember:

**You don't have to be an RSPB member or bank
with The Co-operative Bank to apply.**

Credit facilities are provided by The Co-operative Bank plc, PO Box 101, 1
Balloon Street, Manchester M60 4EP, and are subject to status. Written
quotations are available on request. The Bank may decline any
application. Credit is not available to minors.

BLEAN WOODS,
KENT

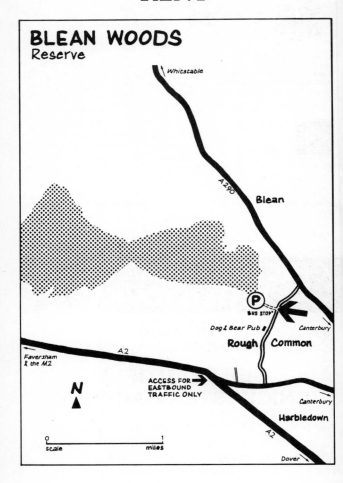

Location

Part of the extensive Blean Forest to the west of Canterbury, Blean Woods is entered, as signposted, at Rough Common. Approaching from the west on the A2, take the first road on the left to Canterbury, then the second turning on the left to Rough Common. From Canterbury, take the A290 road to Whitstable, turning after 1 1/2 miles (2.4 km) for Rough Common. TR/126593. The nearest railway station is Canterbury East (2 miles - 3.2 km).

One of the largest ancient woodlands in Britain and excellent for seeing woodland birds. There are three waymarked paths of varying lengths. Good, level paths provide easy walking throughout the year.

Habitat
The reserve covers 765 acres (310 ha) of mainly deciduous woodland on clay and gravel soil, being part of a larger block of some 2,000 acres (809 ha). Mature oakwood contrasts with open sweet chestnut coppice and areas of silver birch, and is crossed by several rides.

Birds
Green, great spotted and lesser spotted woodpeckers, nightingales, tree pipits, willow warblers, blackcaps, garden warblers and nuthatches all breed here, along with redstarts, hawfinches and wood warblers, which are scarce in south-east England. Crossbills can sometimes be seen.

Other wildlife
One of the few sites of the endangered butterfly, heath fritillary, whose caterpillars feed on the yellow cow-wheat and whose numbers are being increased by habitat management. The butterflies fly on sunny days from mid-June to late July.

Visiting
Access at all times along three waymarked paths of one, two and three miles (3.2 and 5 km) length respectively. Please keep to these paths.

Facilities
P &. **G**

Warden
Michael Walter, 11 Garden Close, Rough Common, Canterbury CT2 9BP.

i 34 St Margaret's Street, Canterbury CT1 2TG (tel: 0227 766567).

DUNGENESS,
KENT

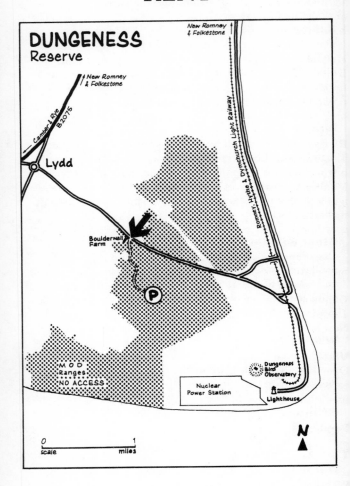

Location

Situated on the large and exposed shingle foreland of Dungeness, the reserve is entered off the straight Lydd to Dungeness road as signposted. TR/063196. The nearest British Rail Station is Rye (10 miles - 16 km). A light railway connects Hythe and Dungeness.

This coastal reserve comprises shingle beach and flooded pits. It is a good place to watch breeding terns, gulls and other waterbirds, migrants and grebes, divers and ducks in the winter. There is 1 1/2 miles of trails, some of which are suitable for wheelchairs and pushchairs, birdwatching hides and an information centre with a seasonal shop.

Habitat

Extensive shingle, part of which has been excavated to form flooded pits which are of high value to waterfowl. Also natural ponds, marshy depressions and scattered clumps of gorse and bramble. The reserve covers 2,106 acres (851 ha).

Birds

The islands of Burrowes Pit have a large nesting colony of common and Sandwich terns with black-headed, Mediterranean and common gulls. Wheatears, great crested and little grebes also nest. Large flocks of teals, shovelers, mallards, pochards and tufted ducks occur outside the breeding season, other winter visitors being goldeneyes, goosanders, smews and both Slavonian and red-necked grebes. Dungeness is famous for small migrants including many rarities.

Other wildlife

The introduced marsh frog is abundant. Viper's bugloss and Nottingham catchfly flower on the shingle.

Visiting

Open daily except Tuesday, 9 am to 9 pm or sunset when earlier. Visitor centre open 10 am - 5 pm; 1 1/2 mile (2.4 km) nature trail and hides.

Facilities

P £ WC IC 🦽 s G ☕

Warden

Peter Makepeace, Boulderwall Farm, Dungeness Road, Lydd, Romney Marsh TN29 9PN.

i 2 Littlestone Road, New Romney, Kent TN28 8PL (tel: 0679 64044).

ELMLEY MARSHES, KENT

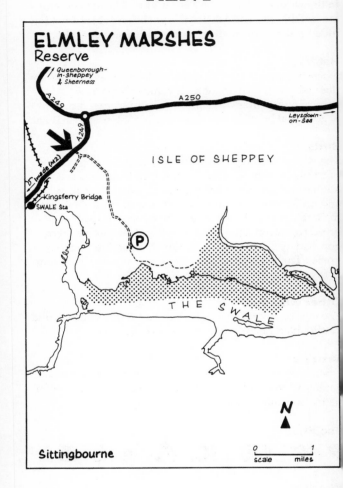

Location

Forming part of the extensive North Kent Marshes, the reserve is reached by taking the long farm track which starts from the A249 road to Sheerness one mile (1.6 km) beyond Kingsferry bridge. TQ/926705. The nearest railway station is in Swale (3 1/2 miles - 5.6 km).

This remote Kent reserve is reached by a 1 1/2 mile (2.5 km) walk from the car park. There are five hides overlooking the flooded areas and saltings. Elmley is an outstanding reserve to watch thousands of wading birds and ducks during the winter, plus excellent for breeding and passage waders and waterfowl.

Habitat

Covering 697 acres (282 ha), the reserve comprises coastal grazing marshes with freshwater fleets and shallow floods, bordered by saltmarsh on the north side of the Swale estuary.

Birds

Habitat management and wardening has made the Spitend peninsula a major refuge for thousands of wigeons, teals, mallards, shelducks and white-fronted geese in winter. The waders include black-tailed godwit, curlew, dunlin and redshank in winter when hen harriers, merlins and short-eared owls occur regularly. In the breeding season redshanks, lapwings, pochards, mallards and shovelers are numerous and both avocets and little terns also nest. Curlew sandpipers, spotted redshanks and rarities such as Kentish plovers use the reserve on passage.

Other wildlife

A rare moth, the ground lackey, occurs in the saltmarsh. Marsh and common frogs, slow-worm and grass snake are all present.

Visiting

Open daily except Tuesday, 9 am to 9 pm or sunset when earlier. The Spitend flooded area and saltings are overlooked by five hides which are reached by a 1 1/2 mile (2.5 km) walk from the reserve car park. (Elderly and disabled visitors are allowed to drive there.) Please keep to the main paths and below the seawall.

Facilities

P £ WC G

Warden

Bob Gomes, Kingshill Farm, Elmley, Sheerness, Isle of Sheppey ME12 3RW.

i Bridge Road Car Park, Sheerness, Kent ME12 1RH (tel: 0795 665324).

FORE WOOD,
EAST SUSSEX

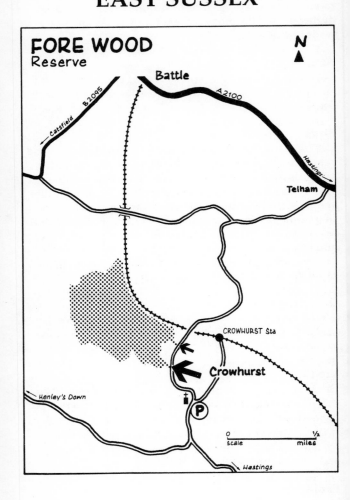

Location

This Wealden woodland lies on the edge of Crowhurst, two miles (3.2 km) south-west of Telham on the A2100 Battle to Hastings road. TQ/756126. The nearest railway station is in Crowhurst (1/4 mile - 400 m).

A simple nature trail explores most of this coppiced woodland. As the paths can be muddy, suitable footwear is recommended.

Habitat
Undulating woodland of coppiced hornbeam and sweet chestnut with oak standards and containing glades, rides, a pond and two ravine (ghyll) streams with waterfalls. The reserve covers 135 acres (55 ha).

Birds
There is a growing number of breeding birds due to habitat improvement including great, marsh and willow tits, great and lesser spotted woodpeckers, spotted flycatchers, chiffchaffs, garden warblers, nightingales and blackcaps. Sparrowhawks and hawfinches also occur.

Other wildlife
Interesting ferns and mosses thrive in the sandstone ghylls. Bluebells, wood anemones and early purple orchids are abundant in spring. White admiral butterflies fly in the rides.

Visiting
Access at all times along a nature trail which explores most of the wood. Visitors are asked to park at Crowhurst village hall opposite the church and to walk up the road to either of the reserve entrances.

Facilities
P

Warden
Martin Allison, Crown House, Petteridge Lane, Matfield, Tonbridge, Kent TN12 7LT.

i 88 High Street, Battle, East Sussex TN33 0QA (tel: 042 773721).

LANGSTONE HARBOUR, HAMPSHIRE

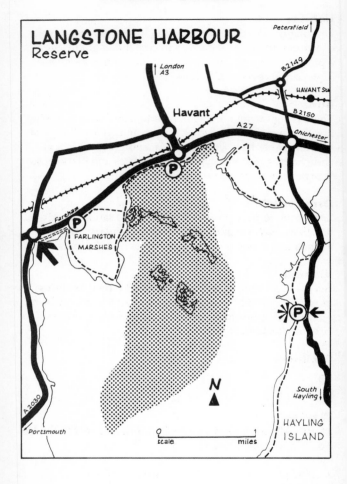

Location

Occupying a central portion of Langstone Harbour, the reserve's low islands and mudflats may be viewed from the coastal footpath along the northern shore, also from the seawall of Farlington Marshes (a reserve of the Hampshire and Isle of Wight Wildlife Trust). The nearest railway station is in the town of Havant.

While there is no access to this reserve, good views can be obtained from a number of viewpoints and car parks.

Habitat
Mudflats and creeks with saltmarsh and shingle islands covering 1,370 acres (554 ha).

Birds
The islands are the site of one of Britain's largest little tern colonies. Common terns, ringed plovers and redshanks also breed there. The entire harbour is outstanding for wintering wildfowl including over 7,000 brent geese as well as teals, wigeons, shelducks, dunlins, oystercatchers, curlews and black-tailed godwits. Black-necked grebes, red-breasted mergansers and greenshanks occur regularly outside the breeding season.

Other wildlife
Areas of saltmarsh and shingle plants.

Visiting
There is no official reserve entrance but there are good views from the car park close to the roundabout at the junction of the A3 and A27 (SU/698057) and at the car park off the Hayling Island road by the Esso garage (SU/718029). Access to Farlington Marshes and good viewpoints may be gained from the roundabout at the junction of the A2030 and A27 Chicester to Fareham road (SU/675043). The reserve islands are subject to a restricted landing policy: the southern end of Long Island is open at all times and Round Nap outside the breeding season, all other areas being closed.

NB Groups wishing to visit Farlington Marshes should book, well in advance, with the Hampshire and Isle of Wight Wildlife Trust warden, 71 The Hundred, Romsey, Hants SO51 8BZ (tel: 0794 513786).

Warden
Andy Polkey, 46 Stein Road, Southbourne, Emsworth, Hampshire PO10 8LD.

i The Hard, Portsmouth, Hampshire PO1 3QJ (tel: 0705 826722).

NOR MARSH and MOTNEY HILL,

KENT

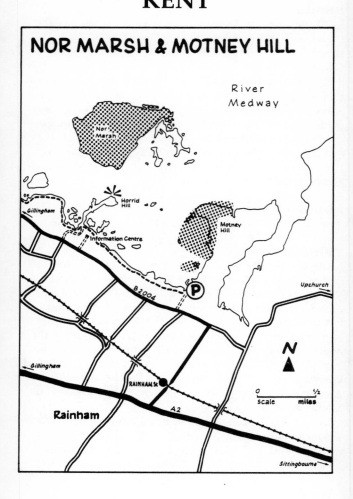

Location

Forming part of the Medway Estuary, these two areas lie east of Gillingham and are reached via the B2004 Lower Rainham Road out of Chatham. The nearest railway stations are Gillingham (3 miles - 4.8 km) and Rainham (2 miles - 3.2 km).

This estuary reserve can be seen well from the viewpoint at Riverside Country Park overlooking Nor Marsh.

Habitat

Saltmarsh and intertidal mud covering 251 acres (101 ha).

Birds

Common terns nest on the island of Nor Marsh where little and Sandwich terns occur in autumn. The saltings and tidal water off Motney Hill attract numerous great crested and some rarer grebes in winter together with brent geese, goldeneyes, red-breasted mergansers and pintails. Waders are abundant including many black-tailed godwits in spring and autumn and whimbrels on passage.

Other wildlife

Essex skipper butterflies, short-winged coneheads and Roesel's bush crickets are some of the more interesting insects.

Visiting

Nor Marsh can be viewed from the end of Horrid Hill (TQ/811689), with parking in the Riverside Country Park. Visitors must not walk out over the old causeway to the island. Access at all times to the seawall and edge of the bay by Motney Hill by driving down Motney Hill Road and using the small car park on the left (TQ/82680) - but not farther along the private road please.

Warden

Alan Parker, Swigshole Cottage, High Halstow, Rochester ME3 8SR.

i Eastgate Cottage, High Street, Rochester ME1 1EW (tel: 0634 843666).

NORTHWARD HILL,
KENT

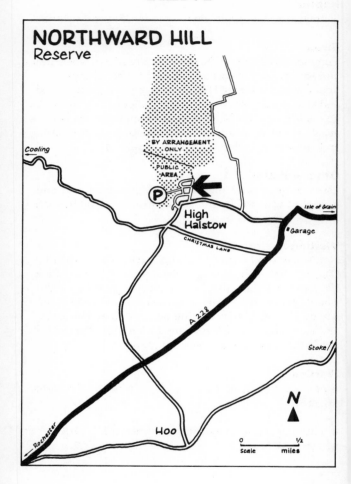

Location

Overlooking the Thames Marshes north of Rochester, the reserve lies on rising ground at the edge of High Halstow which is reached via the A228 road to the Isle of Grain. Then follow the brown road signs in High Halstow village. TQ/784759. The nearest railway station is in Rochester (6 miles - 9.6 km).

A small but very impressive woodland for birds, including Britain's largest heronry. Following an extension to the reserve in 1992, trails and hides are being developed to provide easy access and good views. Before visiting phone the regional office (0273 463642) for an update on progress.

Habitat

Deciduous woodland of oak, ash and maple with elm scrub and dense thickets of hawthorn, together with wet grassland. The reserve covers 623 acres (252 ha).

Birds

The location of Britain's largest heronry of some 220 pairs which feed on the marshes below. Many nightingales and turtle doves breed, as well as whitethroats, lesser whitethroats, garden warblers, blackcaps and both great and lesser spotted woodpeckers. Merlins and sparrowhawks frequently prey on the thrush roosts in winter.

Other wildlife

A thriving colony of white-letter hairstreak butterflies occupies the elm scrub. Essex skipper and speckled wood butterflies also occur.

Visiting

The paths in the public part of the reserve are accessible at all times. Escorted parties to the northern part of the reserve by arrangement with the warden.

Warden

Alan Parker, Swigshole Cottage, High Halstow, Rochester ME3 8SR.

i Eastgate Cottage, High Street, Rochester ME1 1EW (tel: 0634 843666).

Grey heron

PILSEY ISLAND,
WEST SUSSEX

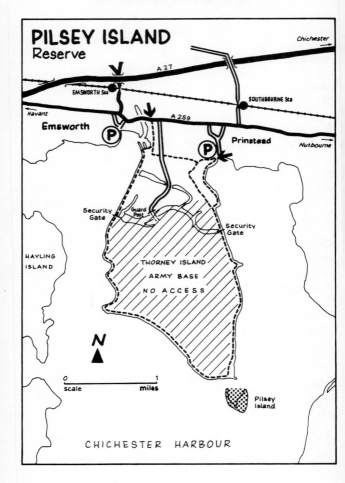

Location

This small island lies off the southern tip of Thorney Island
in the centre of Chichester Harbour. The nearest railway
station is in Emsworth (4 miles - 6.5 km).

While there is no access to the island itself, good views can be obtained from the coastal path around the island. The circuit is seven miles long and suitable footwear is advised. Unfortunately there are no hides or toilets along the path.

Habitat
Forty-five acres (18 ha) of shingle, sand dunes and saltmarsh.

Birds
The site of the largest wader roost in Chichester Harbour, notably of oystercatchers, grey plovers, sanderlings, dunlins and bar-tailed godwits. In winter up to 2,000 brent geese may be seen, with smaller numbers of ducks. Ringed plovers, redshanks and shelducks nest here.

Other wildlife
The plants include sea spurge and yellow-horned poppy.

Visiting
While no visiting is allowed, excellent views of the island and wader roosts can be obtained from Longmere Point (SU/768010) on the coastal footpath around Thorney Island. This path, a seven-mile (11.2 km) circuit, can be reached from Emsworth (car park at SU/749056) or Prinsted (car park at SU/766051).
NB There is strictly no access to Thorney Island Army Base.

Warden
Andy Polkey, 46 Stein Road, Southbourne, Emsworth, Hampshire PO10 8LD.

i St Peter's Market, West Street, Chichester PO19 1AH (tel: 0243 775888).

PULBOROUGH BROOKS,
WEST SUSSEX

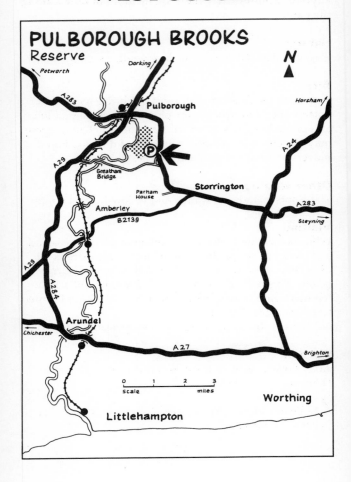

Location

Set in the Arun Valley close to the South Downs, reached via the visitor centre on the A283 at Wiggonholt, between Pulborough (A29 Horsham-Bognor Regis) and Storrington (A24 Horsham-Worthing). TQ/063165. Signposted from Pulborough. The nearest railway station is in Pulborough (2 miles - 3.2 km).

Pulborough Brooks in an excellent reserve for all the family to visit. There are a number of trails and hides, some of which are suitable for wheelchairs and pushchairs. Upperton's Barn Visitor Centre offers informative displays, a shop, tearoom and toilets. A programme of events is available throughout the year.

Habitat

The reserve has 300 acres (121 ha) of water-meadows or 'brooks', with ditches and open water, plus 120 acres (49 ha) of high pasture, hedgerows, mixed woodland, scrub and bracken.

Birds

Breeding birds include garganeys, shovelers, teals, lapwings, snipe, redshanks and yellow wagtails; nightingales and warblers in the scrub and hedges; and nightjars and woodcocks on nearby heathland. Hobbies regularly hunt on the reserve. In winter, Bewick's swans, wigeons and pintails are joined by hen harriers, short-eared owls, and occasional peregrines and merlins. Waders such as whimbrels, spotted redshanks, wood sandpipers, black-tailed godwits and occasional rarities pass through on migration.

Other wildlife

Roe and fallow deer, water voles, adders and grass snakes, at least 23 butterfly and 19 dragonfly species (including the nationally rare club-tailed dragonfly) and many other scarce invertebrates.

Visiting

Open daily: reserve (except 25 December) 9 am - 9 pm (or sunset if earlier); Upperton's Barn Visitor Centre (except 25-26 December) 10 am - 5 pm. Free parking and admission to centre. Wildlife trail, viewpoint and four hides. The visitor centre has a shop and tearoom.

Facilities

P £ WC IC ♿ G S 🍴

Warden

Tim Callaway, Upperton's Barn Visitor Centre, Wiggonholt, Pulborough, West Sussex RH20 2EL.

i All West Sussex Tourist Information Centres including 61 High Street, Arundel BN18 9NJ (tel: 0903 882268).

TUDELEY WOODS, KENT

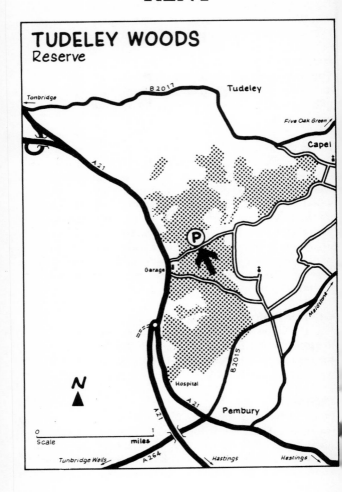

Location

A woodland of the High Weald lying beside the A21
Tonbridge to Hastings road and entered off the minor
road to Capel two miles from Tonbridge. TQ/616433. The
nearest railway station is in Tonbridge (3 miles - 4.8 km).

Set in very attractive deciduous woodland this reserve offers quiet woodland walks along two waymarked paths. This is an excellent place to see woodland birds throughout the year. Some of the paths are quite steep and may be muddy so stout footwear is recommended.

Habitat

Deciduous woodland on Tunbridge Wells Sand and Wealden Clay comprising mature oaks with sweet chestnuts and other coppice; also some grazing pasture. The reserve is 708 acres (287 ha) in size.

Birds

Green, great spotted and lesser spotted woodpeckers are common and nuthatches abundant. Blackcaps, garden warblers, willow warblers and whitethroats inhabit the coppices. Tree pipits and hawfinches occur annually while hobbies, nightjars, crossbills, siskins and long-eared owls may breed occasionally.

Other wildlife

The springtime carpets of bluebell and primrose can be impressive and on the sandier soil several scarce heathland plants thrive in the rides. Seven species of orchid including greater butterfly, bird's-nest and purple helleborine are found in the woodland.

Visiting

Access at all times. Visitors are asked to keep to two waymarked trails.

Facilities

P

Warden

Martin Allison, Crown House, Petteridge Lane, Matfield, Tonbridge, Kent TN12 7LT.

i Monson House, Monson Way, Tunbridge Wells TN1 1LQ (tel: 0892 515675).

BERNEY MARSHES and BREYDON WATER,

NORFOLK

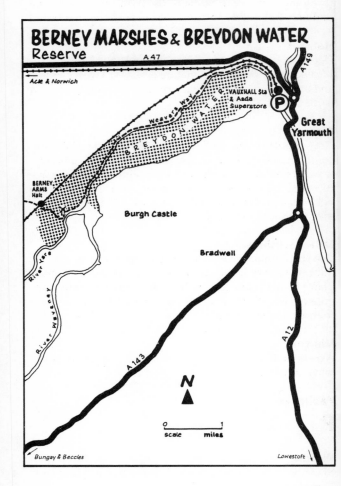

Location

Forming part of the flat, open landscape of Broadland, Berney Marshes and Breydon Water are situated at the confluence of the rivers Yare and Waveney. TG/415055. Berney Arms railway station is next to the reserve.

These two reserves will let you experience the wildlife and wilderness of east Norfolk. Breydon can be reached from Great Yarmouth or the Weavers' Way, while Berney Marsh is best visited by train then walking back to Great Yarmouth (4 miles - 6.4 km). Due to the remoteness of these reserves no facilities are available.

Habitat
1,290 acres (523 ha) of grazing marshes and dykes.

Birds
Flooding has attracted wintering flocks of wigeons, teals, pintails and shelducks, while white-fronted geese and Bewick's swans graze on the marshes. The extensive mudflats of Breydon Water attract many curlews, dunlins and redshanks and other waders.

Other wildlife
The dykes contain an interesting flora and abundant invertebrates including the rare Norfolk aeshna dragonfly.

Visiting
No road access to Berney, but the railway from Yarmouth stops at Berney Arms Halt. The Weavers' Way from Yarmouth (4 miles - 6.4 km) crosses the reserve and passes Breydon Water. Limited car parking at ASDA superstore in Yarmouth. Boat trips are available, details from warden.

Warden
Dave Barrett, Ashtree Farm, Breydon Marine, Butt Lane, Burgh Castle, Great Yarmouth, Norfolk NR31 9PZ.

i Town Hall, Hall Quay, Great Yarmouth NR30 2PX (tel: 0493 846345).

BOYTON MARSHES,
SUFFOLK

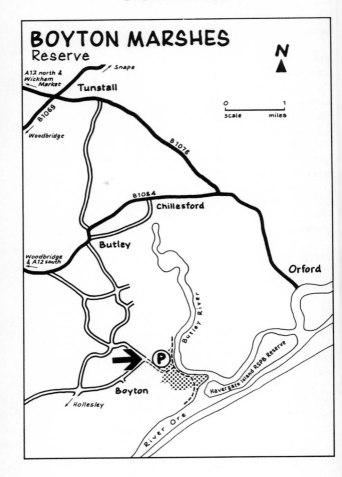

Location

Lying at the junction of Butley River and the River Ore (opposite the southern end of Havergate Island), on the Suffolk coast. TM/390470. The nearest railway station is in Woodbridge (8 miles - 13 km).

Overlooking Havergate Island Reserve, this coastal marsh can be seen from the public footpaths that cross it.

Habitat
Coastal grazing marsh with ditch systems. Substantial saltmarsh borders the reserve on the Butley River side. The reserve is 175 acres (71 ha) in size.

Birds
Reed and sedge warblers, coots, moorhens, and mute swans all breed on the reserve. Nightingales and grasshopper warblers occur most years. Occasional marsh harriers hunt over the reserve. Winter ducks include wigeons and tufted ducks.

Other wildlife
The saltmarsh bordering Butley River has typical saltmarsh plants.

Visiting
Access at all times along the public footpaths. No parking on roadway to the reserve please.

Facilities
P

Warden
John Partridge, 30 Mundays Lane, Orford, Woodbridge, Suffolk IP12 2LX.

i Town Hall, Market Place, Southwold, Suffolk IP18 6EF (tel: 0502 724729).

Moorhen

FOWLMERE,
CAMBRIDGESHIRE

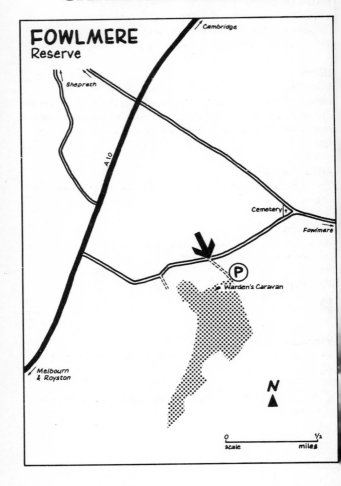

Location

Situated near Fowlmere village, the reserve is reached by turning off the A10 Cambridge to Royston road by Shepreth. TL/407461. The nearest railway station is in Shepreth (3 miles - 4.8 km).

Fowlmere is an ideal reserve for all the family, and particularly children. The trails wind through woodland, reedbeds and old cressbeds. One of the four hides is raised to give excellent views over the reedbed. Part of the trail and one of the hides are suitable for wheelchairs and pushchairs. Unfortunately, there are no toilets on the reserve.

Habitat
An isolated fen of 86 acres (35 ha) within arable farmland comprising reeds and pools fed by spring water; also some hawthorn scrub, an alder copse and deciduous woodland.

Birds
A large colony of reed warblers nests in the reedbeds with sedge warblers, reed buntings, grasshopper warblers and water rails. Kingfishers are seen frequently and green sandpipers occur on migration. Whitethroats and turtle doves nest in the scrub which in autumn and winter is used by large flocks of roosting fieldfares, redwings and corn buntings.

Other wildlife
Southern marsh orchids, autumn gentian, small scabious and cowslips flower in the chalky grass areas. Frogs and toads are abundant in spring. Grass snakes are common.

Visiting
A nature trail incorporates four hides, one of which is elevated. There is a boardwalk trail for disabled visitors near the entrance.

Facilities
P ♿ G

Warden
Mike Pollard, 19 Whitecroft road, Meldreth, Nr Royston, Herts SG8 6ND.

i Wheeler Street, Cambridge CB2 3QB (tel: 0223 322640).

FRAMPTON MARSHES,
LINCOLNSHIRE

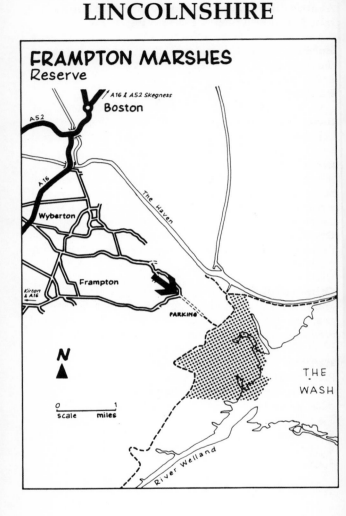

Location

Lying in the south-west corner of The Wash, the reserve is reached by following the signs for Frampton Marsh off the A16 at Kirton. TF/364383. The nearest railway station is in Boston (5 miles - 8 km).

Overlooking The Wash, this is a wide open space to watch thousands of birds especially during the winter. Although there are no hides, good views can be obtained from the seawall.

Habitat
The reserve has 930 acres (376 ha) of mature saltmarsh, partly grazed, leading to a network of creeks and intertidal mudflats.

Birds
The saltmarsh holds one of the densest concentrations of nesting redshanks in Britain. Thousands of brent geese frequent these marshes and flats in winter with shelducks, wigeons and numerous dunlins, knots and redshanks. Hen harriers, short-eared owls, sparrowhawks and merlins all occur in the winter.

Other wildlife
Saltmarsh plants including sea aster and sea wormwood.

Visiting
Cars may drive down the access track but must park on the grass verge out of the way of farm machinery. There are good birdwatching sites along the seawall but the saltmarsh itself should not be entered because of dangerous creeks.

Warden
Present from April to February, c/o The Post Office, Frampton, nr Boston, Lincolnshire. At other times enquiries to Snettisham warden (page 97).

i Blackfriars Arts Centre, Spain Lane, Boston PE21 6HP (tel: 0205 356656).

Hen harrier

HAVERGATE ISLAND, SUFFOLK

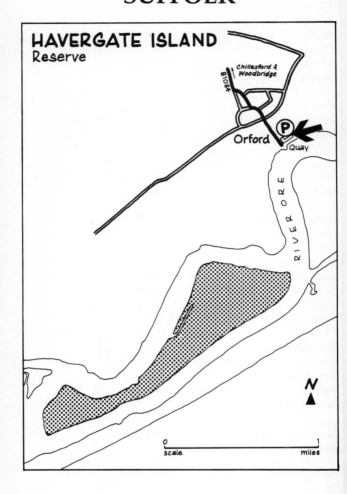

Location

Lying within the River Ore on the Suffolk coast, the island is reached by boat from Orford quay. TM/425496. The nearest railway station is in Woodbridge (11 miles - 17.5 km).

Havergate is a low-lying island reached by boat from Orford between April and August. There are limited facilities on the island, including several hides and basic toilets.

Habitat

A low embanked island in the River Ore containing shallow, brackish water lagoons with islands and surrounded by saltmarsh and shingle beaches. The reserve is 267 acres (108 ha) in size.

Birds

Britain's largest nesting colony of avocets was established here in 1947 and now numbers some 120 pairs. Sandwich and common terns, oystercatchers, ringed plovers, redshanks and shelducks also breed and several wader species occur on passage. Many avocets remain over winter when teals, wigeons, pintails, shovelers, mallards and occasionally Bewick's swans and hen harriers are present.

Other wildlife

Sea purslane and sea lavender flower on the saltings and sea pea and English stonecrop on the shingle beach. Roesel's bush cricket is a speciality in late summer.

Visiting

Boat trips are run to the island between April and August on the first and third Saturdays and Sundays of each month and every Thursday, leaving Orford quay at 10 am and 11.30 am. Please write to the warden enclosing an SAE for your tickets. (Charge: members £3, non-members £5.) Visiting during September - March is on the first Saturday and Sunday of each month. There are several hides as well as an information centre, basic toilets and a picnic area on the island.

Facilities

IC   G

Warden

John Partridge, 30 Mundays Lane, Orford, Woodbridge IP12 2LX.

i The Cinema, High Street, Aldeburgh, Suffolk (tel: 0728 453637).

MINSMERE,
SUFFOLK

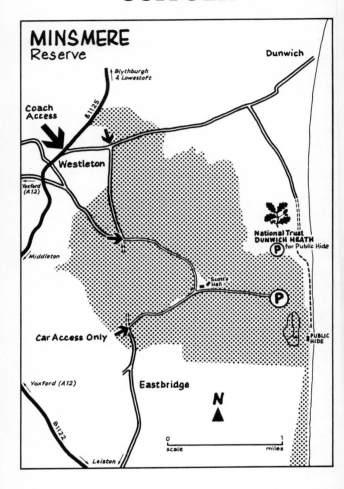

Location

Lying on the low Suffolk coast, this premier RSPB reserve is reached either from Westleton or through East Bridge (no coaches this way) from the B1122 road from Leiston to Yoxford. It is clearly signposted in the vicinity. TM/452680. The nearest railway station is in Saxmundham (6 miles - 9.6 km).

Minsmere is one of the RSPB's most popular nature reserves. It is famous for its nesting avocets, marsh harriers and bitterns. It offers many opportunities for visitors, both families and birdwatchers alike. There are countryside walks of varying lengths and seven hides. Most of the paths are suitable for wheelchairs and pushchairs. Car parking, shop, toilets and snacks are available. The reserve is closed on Tuesdays.

Habitat
The famous Scrape - an area of shallow brackish water, mud and islands - as well as extensive reedbeds with meres, heathland, woodland, grazing marsh and dunes. The reserve covers 2,016 acres (816 ha).

Birds
A large variety of breeding birds includes common terns and Britain's second largest avocet colony on the Scrape; little terns on the beach; bitterns, marsh harriers, bearded tits and water rails in the reeds; nightjars and stonechats on the heath and nightingales and redstarts in the woods. Many different waders such as spotted redshank, black-tailed godwit, little stint and several rarities use the Scrape on migration. Bewick's swans, white-fronted geese, wigeons, gadwalls and teals occur in winter.

Other wildlife
Water voles and otters frequent the marshes, red deer and muntjac the woods, while adders and silver-studded blue butterflies are found on the heath.

Visiting
Open daily, 9 am to 9 pm or sunset when earlier, except Tuesdays. Car drivers are asked to take special care on the narrow lanes within and approaching the reserve. The public hide on the beach overlooking the Scrape is always open (free of charge) and is reached on foot from Dunwich Cliffs National Trust car park (TM/475680).

Facilities
P £ WC IC ♿ G S ☕

Warden
Geoff Welch, Minsmere Reserve, Westleton, Saxmundham IP17 3BY (tel: 072 873 281).

i Town Hall, High Street, Southwold, Suffolk IP18 6EF (tel: 0502 724729).

NENE WASHES,
CAMBRIDGESHIRE

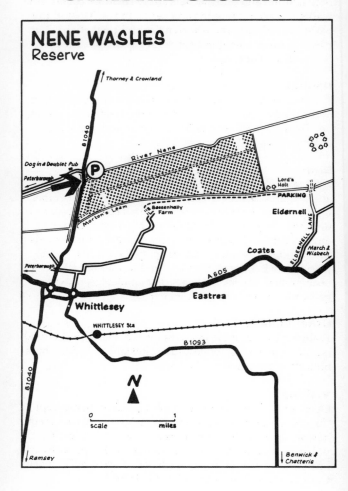

Location

This Fenland reserve is situated five miles (8 km) east of Peterborough and is entered off the B1040 road from Whittlesey to Thorney. TL/277992. The nearest railway station is in Whittlesey (2 miles - 3.2 km).

Although there are currently no facilities for visitors, the reserve can be seen from the drove.

Habitat

The reserve covers 715 acres (289 ha) of washland, mostly wet meadows with marsh and ditches lying between the River Nene and Morton's Leam.

Birds

Black-tailed godwits, lapwings, redshanks, snipe, sedge warblers, yellow wagtails, shovelers, mallards, gadwalls, garganeys, tufted ducks and shelducks all nest regularly. Marsh harriers and hobbies occur in summer, and hen harriers and merlins in winter. A variety of waders, such as ruff, green sandpiper, whimbrel and greenshank occur on migration. When flooding happens in winter, large flocks of Bewick's swans, wigeons, teals, shovelers and pintails visit the reserve.

Other wildlife

Greater bladderwort, flowering rush, frogbit and water violet flower in the ditches which support several dragonfly species.

Visiting

There are currently no facilities but there is access along the drove. There is no access to the fields.

Facilities

P

Warden

Charlie Kitchin, 32 Pinewood Avenue, Whittlesey, Cambridgeshire PE7 1EU.

i Town Hall, Bridge Street, Peterborough, Cambridgeshire PE1 1HA (tel: 0733 317336, weekdays only 63141).

NORTH WARREN,
SUFFOLK

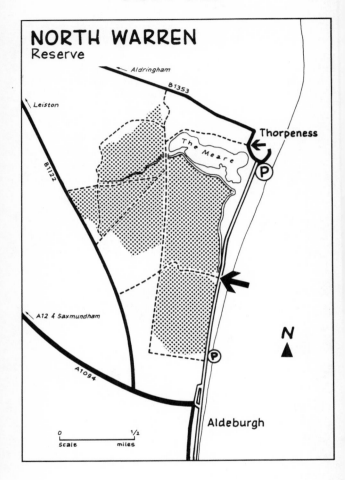

Location

Lying on the Suffolk coast on the banks of the Hundred River, the reserve can be entered on foot from Thorpeness and Aldeburgh. Car parking is available at Thorpeness TM/472595 and on the north side of Aldeburgh TM/466575. Extensive views of the marshes are available from the coast road. The nearest railway station is in Saxmundham (6 miles - 9.5 km).

A number of simple public footpaths cross this reserve, which is just to the north of Aldeburgh.

Habitat
Coastal grazing marshes with reedbeds, deciduous woodland and acid grassland heath covering 506 acres (205 ha).

Birds
Shelducks, gadwalls, teals, shovelers, lapwings, snipe, redshanks, kingfishers and yellow wagtails all breed regularly with garganeys and ruffs usually present in spring. Spotted redshanks, greenshanks and wood sandpipers occur on migration while in the winter shallow flooding attracts large flocks of Bewick's swans, white-fronted geese, wigeons, gadwalls, pintails, teals and shovelers. Woodlarks, whitethroats and yellowhammers breed on the heath, nightingales in the woodland scrub and reed and sedge warblers along the dykes.

Other wildlife
Adders, green hairstreak and grayling butterflies occur on the heath, purple hairstreak in the woods and plants such as purple loosestrife, bog bean and yellow rattle flower in the fen.

Visiting
Public footpaths cross the reserve and are accessible at all times.

Facilities
P

Warden
Rob Macklin, Race Walk, Priory Road, Snape, Saxmundham, Suffolk IP17 1SD.

i The Cinema, High Street, Aldeburgh, Suffolk IP15 5AU (tel: 0728 453637).

Yellow wagtail

OLD HALL MARSHES, ESSEX

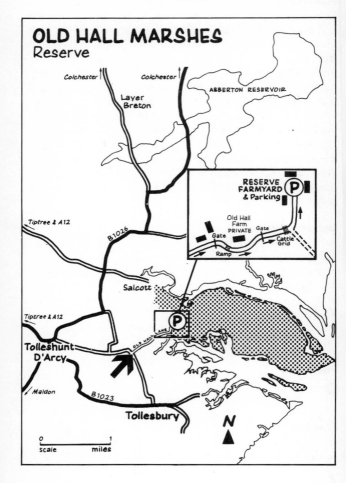

Location

This remote peninsula at the mouth of the Blackwater Estuary is entered at its western end from the minor road between Tollesbury and Tolleshunt D'Arcy. TL/950117. The nearest railway station is in Kelvedon (9 miles - 14.5 km).

To visit this reserve, all visitors must write to the warden in advance.

Habitat
Extensive grazing marshes with brackish water fleets and reedbeds, saltings and two small offshore islands covering 1,560 acres (631 ha).

Birds
In winter, 4,000 brent geese feed on the pasture, with small flocks of ruffs and golden plovers. Thousands of wigeons, teals, shelducks, grey plovers, curlews, redshanks and dunlins frequent the marshes. Divers, grebes, goldeneyes and occasional seaducks are seen on the channels. Short-eared owls, hen harriers, barn owls and merlins regularly hunt the reserve. Breeding species include lapwing, redshank, pochard, shoveler, bearded tit, common tern and corn bunting. During migration, marsh harriers, wheatears, whinchats and waders such as whimbrel, avocet, godwits and stints can be seen.

Other wildlife
The ancient grassland is characterised by thousands of anthills of the yellow meadow ant. The saltmarsh, seawall and brackish water ditches support many unusual plant species. Twenty-two species of butterfly have been recorded. Dragonflies include good numbers of ruddy darter.

Visiting
Please write in advance to the warden for tickets to visit the reserve. The reserve is open daily except Tuesdays from 9 am to 9 pm (or sunset when earlier). Car drivers are asked to take special care on the narrow approach lane with its 20 mph speed restriction. Drive a quarter of a mile (1.6 km) beyond Old Hall Farm to reach the reserve.

Facilities
P

Warden
Chris Tyas, 1 Old Hall Lane, Tolleshunt D'Arcy, Maldon, Essex CM9 8TP.

i Maritime Centre, The Hythe, Maldon, Essex (tel: 0621 856503).

Dunlin

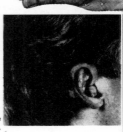

OUSE WASHES,
CAMBRIDGESHIRE

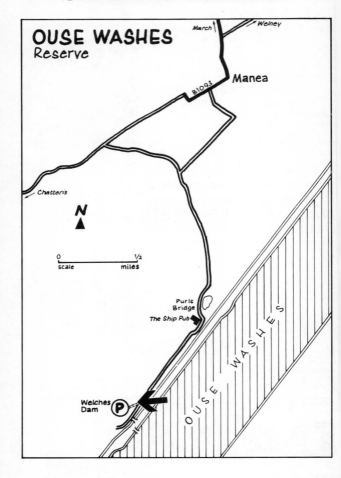

Location

Part of a 19-mile (30 km) stretch of flood washland, the RSPB reserve is entered at Welches Dam which is signposted from Manea village. Approach via the B1093 or B1098 roads from the A141 road from Chatteris to March. TL/471861. The nearest railway station is in Manea (3 miles - 4.8 km).

The Ouse Washes are known for the waterbirds and particularly whooper and Bewick's swans that spend the winter there. Hides give good views over the reserve. There is an information centre with toilets.

Habitat
Extensive wet meadowland or 'washes', dissected by many ditches and contained by two parallel rivers that were excavated in the 17th century. Several osier beds grow by the River Delph. The reserve totals 2,083 acres (850 ha).

Birds
Black-tailed godwits nest, their success depending on the state of flooding in the spring. Ruffs 'lek' annually and may nest; other breeding species include shoveler, teal, garganey, yellow wagtail, lapwing, redshank and snipe. In winter, when the washes are flooded, the reserve is the most important site inland in Britain for wildfowl including Bewick's swans and huge numbers of wigeons, teals, pintails and mallards as well as shovelers, whooper swans, hen harriers and merlins.

Other wildlife
A rich variety of aquatic plants includes fringed water-lily, flowering rush, brooklime and arrowhead.

Visiting
Access at all times from the reserve car park, with an information centre (open weekends and Bank holidays) and toilets, to a series of hides (provided by the RSPB and the Bedfordshire and Cambridgeshire Wildlife Trust) overlooking the washes. Visitors are requested to walk below and behind the bank to avoid disturbing the birds.

Facilities
P WC IC G s

Warden
Cliff Carson, Limosa, Welches Dam, Manea, March PE15 0ND.

i Oliver Cromwell's House, 29 St Mary's Street, Ely, Cambridgeshire CB7 4HF (tel: 0353 662062).

SNETTISHAM,
NORFOLK

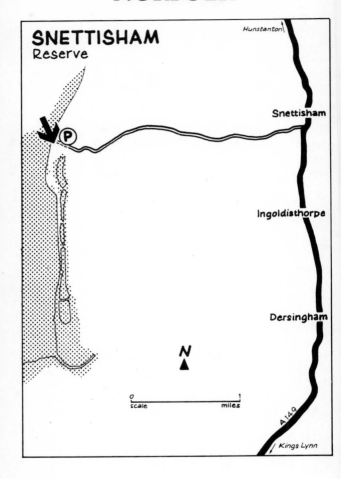

Location

Occupying part of the east shore of the Wash, the beach and reserve are reached from Snettisham village on the A149 road from King's Lynn to Hunstanton. TF/648335. The nearest railway station is in Kings Lynn (12 miles - 19 km).

Snettisham is an excellent place to watch hundreds of thousands of birds flying over the mudflats and onto the reserve to roost especially at high tides. There are four hides and spectacular open views of sea, sky and birds. The farthest hide is two miles from the car park along the beach. Visitors with special needs can drive to the hide at the eastern end of the reserve.

Habitat

A shingle beach containing flooded pits borders a vast expanse of tidal sand and mudflats with saltmarsh. The reserve is 3,257 acres (1,316 ha) in size.

Birds

In winter up to 130,000 waders roost near the beach and on the artificial islands in the pit during high tides. These include knots, grey plovers, bar-tailed godwits, oystercatchers, dunlins, redshanks, curlews, turnstones and ringed plovers. Thousands of pink-footed and brent geese with shelducks, mallards, wigeons, pintails and teals use the foreshore for feeding and roosting. Diving ducks such as red-breasted mergansers, tufted ducks and scaups also frequent the pits which in summer have a nesting colony of common terns. Large numbers of sanderlings and several passerines such as wheatear pause on migration.

Other wildlife

The shingle beach flora includes yellow-horned poppy, sea beet and hoary mullein.

Visiting

Access at all times to the reserve beach and four hides to which visitors are required to walk (passing the holiday chalets) from the public car park. Cars with disabled visitors and by arrangement with the warden may drive down and through the reserve gate at the southern end of the chalets.

Facilities

P IC & G s

Warden

Paul Fisher, 13 Beach Road, Snettisham, King's Lynn, Norfolk PE31 7RA.

i The Green, Hunstanton, Norfolk PE36 5AH
(tel: 0485 32610).

STOUR ESTUARY, ESSEX

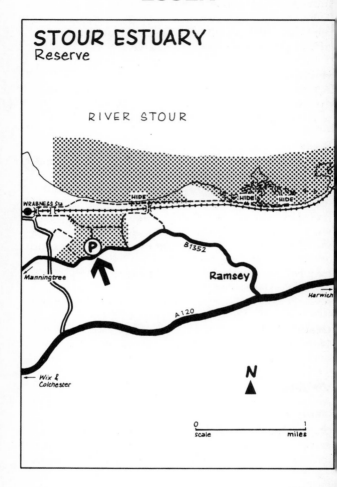

STOUR ESTUARY
Reserve

RIVER STOUR

WRABNESS Sta.

HIDE HIDE HIDE

P

B1352

Manningtree

Ramsey

Harwich

A120

← Wix &
Colchester

N

0		1
scale		miles

Location

Including most of Copperas Bay in the south-east of the
Stour Estuary west of Harwich, the reserve is entered in
Stour Wood off the B1352 road from Manningtree to Ramsey
one mile (1.6 km) east of Wrabness Village. TM/189309.
The nearest railway station is in Wrabness (1 mile - 1.6 km).

This is a woodland and estuary reserve. There are several walks through the wood, leading to the Stour Estuary, where there are three hides. Due to often damp conditions suitable footwear is advisable.

Habitat
The woodland is predominantly of oak and sweet chestnut with extensive chestnut coppice that is cut rotationally. Copperas Bay contains mudflats fringed by a little saltmarsh, reedbed and scrubby fields. The reserve totals 872 acres (353 ha).

Birds
Nightingales, garden warblers, blackcaps, lesser whitethroats and both great and lesser spotted woodpeckers inhabit the woods and scrub. In autumn and winter wigeons, teals, pintails, shelducks, brent geese, redshanks, curlews, grey plovers and a large flock of black-tailed godwits feed in the bay.

Other wildlife
Butcher's broom, yellow archangel and wild service tree occur in Stour Wood, with dormice and a colony of white admiral butterflies.

Visiting
Access at all times along waymarked paths which lead from the car park through Stour Wood to three hides overlooking the bay - a round trip of four miles (6.4 km). Best birdwatching is from hides in September - April when wading birds are present in the estuary.

Facilities

P

Warden
Russell Leavett, 24 Orchard Close, Great Oakley, Harwich CO12 5AX.

i Parkeston Quay, Harwich, Essex CO12 4SP (tel: 0255 506139).

STRUMPSHAW FEN, NORFOLK

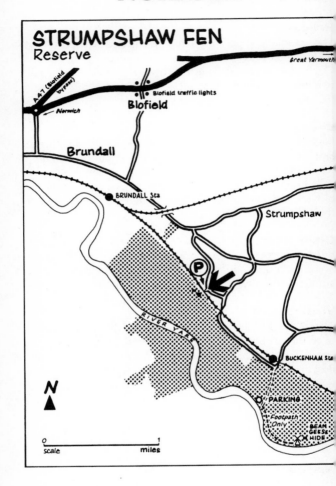

Location

Situated in the Yare Valley in the southern part of the Broads, the reserve is reached from the A47 Norwich to Yarmouth road by turning through Brundall. Beyond the railway bridge turn sharp right and right again into Low Road which leads to the reserve car park. To reach the reception hide, visitors must cross the level-crossing on foot with care. TG/342066. The nearest railway station is in Brundall (2 miles - 3.2 km).

This reserve is in the heart of the Norfolk Broads. A number of walks encircle the fen with views of marsh harriers and swallowtail butterflies. During the early summer a special trail leads you through some excellent flower rich meadows. There is an information point and toilets.

Habitat

A large fen with reed and sedge beds, alder and willow stands, damp woodland and two broads beside the River Yare; also wet grazing marshes. The reserve covers 686 acres (277 ha).

Birds

Marsh harriers, bearded tits, Cetti's warblers, kingfishers, pochards, water rails, great crested grebes, gadwalls, tufted ducks and reed warblers nest in the fen, with redshanks, snipe and yellow wagtails in the marshes. Woodcocks, nuthatches, treecreepers and the three species of woodpeckers frequent the woodland. The largest flock of bean geese in Britain occurs in winter, notably on the adjacent Buckenham Marshes.

Other wildlife

Swallowtail butterflies are seen, especially in June. Chinese water deer, grass snakes and 20 species of dragonflies are present. Marsh pea, purple loosestrife and marsh sow-thistle flower in the fen.

Visiting

Open daily from 9 am to 9 pm or sunset when earlier. A waymarked path encircles the fen and includes three hides (one of which is elevated). Another hide with information displays overlooks the main broad. Fen nature trails interpret the diverse wildlife from late June to August. From November to February a hide is open by the Buckenham Marshes from which to watch the bean geese and wigeons. It is reached over the level-crossing at Buckenham station. (TG/354045).

Facilities

P £ WC IC ♿ G

Warden

Mike Blackburn, Staithe Cottage, Low Road, Strumpshaw, Norwich NR13 4HS.

i The Guildhall, Gaol Hill, Norwich NR2 1NF (tel: 0603 666071).

SURLINGHAM CHURCH MARSH,

NORFOLK

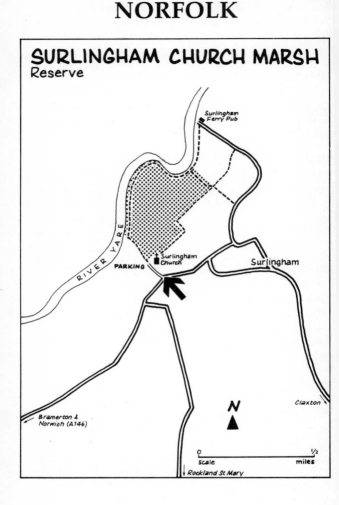

Location

Lying on the south bank of the Yare river, the reserve is entered on foot from Surlingham church which is reached off the A146 road from Norwich to Lowestoft. TG/306064. The nearest railway station is Norwich (6 miles - 9.6 km).

This small Broadland reserve offers pleasant walks along dykes and by reedbeds and pools. There are two hides, but no other facilities.

Habitat
A former grazing marsh containing dykes and pools with reed, sedge, and some alder and willow scrub covering 68 acres (28 ha).

Birds
Little ringed plovers, common terns, shelducks, gadwalls, teals, shovelers and tufted ducks, reed, sedge and grasshopper warblers all breed. Cuckoos are plentiful, and marsh harriers hunt regularly over the marsh. Passage waders include green and wood sandpipers and greenshank. Hen harriers and jack snipe are regular winter visitors; on winter evenings there is a spectacular roost when geese, ducks, lapwings and wagtails gather in their hundreds.

Other wildlife
Wetland plants include frogbit, bog bean, early and southern marsh orchids, marsh cinquefoil and water avens. Dragonflies are numerous in late summer.

Visiting
Access at all times along the waymarked paths from which two hides overlook the marsh and pools. Please park carefully by the church where space is limited.

Warden
Peter Bradley, 2 Chapel Cottages, The Green, Surlingham, Norwich NR14 7AG.

i The Guildhall, Gaol Hill, Norwich (tel: 0603 666071).

TETNEY MARSHES,
LINCOLNSHIRE

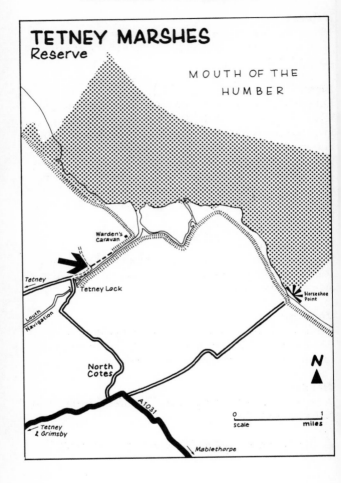

Location

Lying near the mouth of the Humber estuary, the reserve is
entered on foot via the locked entrance gate or the riverbank
east of Tetney lock. This is east of Tetney village which is
on the A1031 south from Cleethorpes. TA/345025. The
nearest railway station is in Cleethorpes (8 miles - 12.8 km).

While there are no formal facilities at Tetney, good views of the reserve are obtained from the seawall overlooking the Humber Estuary.

Habitat
Extensive sandflats bordered by low sand dunes and a wide saltmarsh with creeks covering 3,111 acres (1,258 ha).

Birds
Little terns nest at the tide's edge; shelducks, oystercatchers, ringed plovers and redshanks also breed. Several migrant species occur, including whimbrel. Wigeon, teal, brent goose, oystercatcher, grey and golden plover, bar-tailed godwit and knot flock in winter.

Other wildlife
Grey seals may be seen occasionally.

Visiting
Access at all times. Good views are obtained from the seawall, especially at high tide. Visitors should avoid the saltmarsh and sand dunes because of the dangerous tides. Please do not disturb the little tern colony.

Warden
Present from April to August, c/o The Post Office, Tetney, Grimsby, South Humberside. Other enquiries to RSPB East Anglia Office (page 295).

i 42-43 Alexandra Road, Cleethorpes, Humberside DN35 8LE (tel: 0472 200220).

Wigeons

TITCHWELL MARSH, NORFOLK

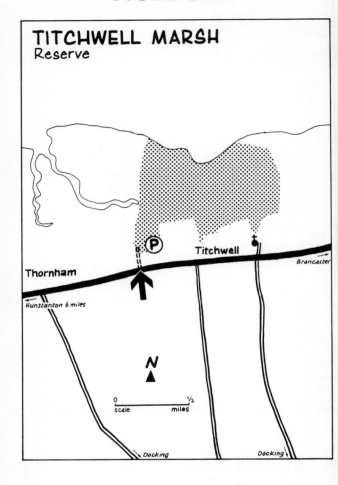

Location

One of a series of nature reserves on the north Norfolk coast, Titchwell is located six miles (9.6 km) east of Hunstanton on the A149 road to Brancaster. Enter the reserve car park between Thornham and Titchwell villages. TF/749436. The nearest railway station is King's Lynn (6 miles - 9.6 km).

This is one of the RSPB's most popular coastal reserves at all times of the year, be it for summer avocets or wintering waders and wildfowl. A firm path takes you to three hides and onto the beach where there is a platform overlooking the sea suitable for wheelchairs. There is a visitor centre with snacks and toilets.

Habitat

Both tidal and freshwater reedbeds, sea aster saltmarsh, brackish and freshwater pools with sand dunes and a shingle beach totalling 510 acres (206 ha).

Birds

A colony of avocets nests on the enclosed marsh with gadwalls, tufted ducks, shovelers and black-headed gulls, while bearded tits, water rails, bitterns and marsh harriers are found in the reedbeds. Common and little terns, ringed plovers and oystercatchers nest on the beach where large flocks of waders roost during the highest autumn tides. During that season many migrants visit the marsh including wigeon, black-tailed godwit, curlew sandpiper and occasional rarities. In winter, brent geese and goldeneyes occur regularly with divers, grebes and seaducks offshore and snow buntings foraging on the beach.

Visiting

Access at all times along the west bank to two hides overlooking the marsh and a third hide overlooking the shingle bank. Visitor centre is open daily (except Christmas), 10 am to 5 pm (4 pm November - March).

Facilities

P £ (car park) **WC IC** ♿ **G S** ☕

Warden

Norman Sills, Titchwell Marsh Reserve, Titchwell, King's Lynn, Norfolk PE31 8BB.

i The Green, Hunstanton, Norfolk PE36 5AH (tel: 0485 532610).

Arctic tern

"THE PHEASANT"

HOTEL AND RESTAURANT

On the Coast Road, Kelling, Norfolk NR25 7EG
Tel: 0263 70382
(From July 1994: 0263 588382)

3 miles East of Cley Reserves
Adjacent to the establishing Kelling Quags

Delightful Country House Hotel set in three acres of
wooded grounds in the tranquillity of rural Norfolk.
The ideal base for visiting Norfolk's famous Reserves.

**30 en-suite bedrooms, with Colour TV
Satellite, Radios, Alarms, Direct Dial Telephones
Tea/Coffee making facilities,
Full Central Heating**

Freehouse: Open to Non-Residents
Bar Meals: Every Day Noon – 2 pm
Restaurant: Every Day 7 pm – 9 pm

BED AND BREAKFAST

Fantastic Value

Rates per person per night including VAT
From 1 November 93 to 31 March 94
(Excluding Christmas and New Year's Eve)

Double Occupancy £20.00
Single Occupancy £25.00

From 1 April 94 to 25 May 94
Double Occupancy £25.00
Single Occupancy £30.00

From 26 May 94
Double Occupancy £30.00
Single Occupancy £36.00

*10% discount for stays of seven or
more consecutive nights*

**North Norfolk Tourism Award
for excellence in Service to tourism**

WOLVES WOOD,
SUFFOLK

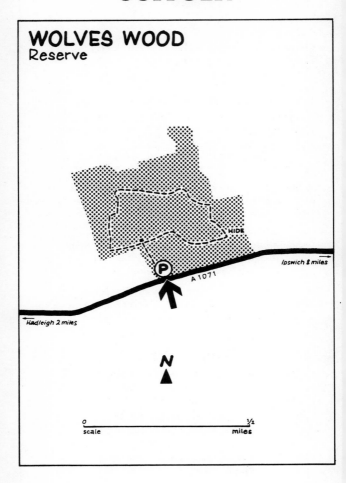

Location

This wood lies beside the A1071 road to Ipswich two miles (3.2 km) east of Hadleigh, in Suffolk farmland. TM/054436. The nearest railway station is in Ipswich (8 miles - 12.8 km).

This small woodland reserve offers woodland walks, with nightingales in spring. There is a small information centre.

Habitat
A mixed deciduous wood of oak, ash, birch, hornbeam, aspen and hazel with an area of coppiced scrub covering 92 acres (37 ha).

Birds
There are many nightingales in the scrub and coppiced rides. Garden warblers, blackcaps, chiffchaffs, willow warblers, nuthatches, great and lesser spotted woodpeckers, marsh and long-tailed tits, woodcocks and occasionally hawfinches all breed on the reserve.

Other wildlife
Herb paris and yellow archangel indicate this wood's ancient origin.

Visiting
Access at all times around the waymarked trail from the car park.

Facilities

P IC G

Warden
None usually present. Enquiries to Russell Leavett, Stour Estuary (page 99).

i Town Hall, Princes Street, Ipswich, Suffolk IP1 1BZ (tel: 0473 258070).

CHURCH WOOD,
BUCKINGHAMSHIRE

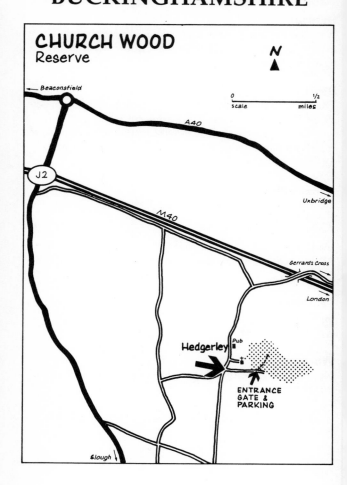

Location

Situated beside the Chilterns village of Hedgerley which is reached from the M40 or A40 intersections near Beaconsfield, turning south on the A355 road to Slough. Immediately south of the M40 turn left for Hedgerley village where a private track to the reserve is entered beside the pond beyond the public house. SU/968873. The nearest railway station is Gerrards Cross (4 miles - 6 km).

A small woodland reserve within the extensive Chiltern woodlands. It has simple waymarked paths.

Habitat

Mixed woodland of 34 acres (14 ha) with mature beech, ash and oak as well as birch, alder and hazel coppice, forming part of the more extensive Chiltern woods.

Birds

Nuthatches, the three species of British woodpeckers, stock doves, blackcaps and several species of tits nest in this woodland.

Other wildlife

Fox and muntjac deer occur as do both white admiral and purple hairstreak butterflies. Butcher's broom and green helleborine are among the plants.

Visiting

Access at all times along waymarked paths which encircle the wood. Please park beside the track to the field gate and entrance to avoid impeding farm traffic.

Warden

None present. Enquiries to RSPB Central England Office (page 295).

i Central Library, St Ives Road, Maidenhead, Berkshire SL6 1QU (tel: 0628 781110).

Blackcap

HIGHNAM WOODS, GLOUCESTERSHIRE

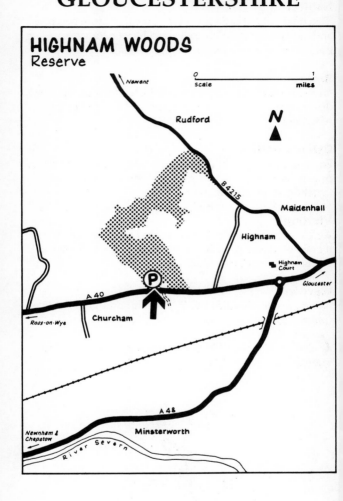

Location

Lying in the Severn Vale, three miles (5.5 km) west of Gloucester, this woodland is entered from the A40 Gloucester to Ross-on-Wye Road at SO/778190. The nearest railway station is in Gloucester (3 1/2 miles - 5.5 km).

With its carpets of bluebells and cowslips this is an ideal reserve to visit in the spring when nightingales can be heard. There are a number of waymarked paths (which can be muddy) and a hide which is accessible to wheelchairs.

Habitat
Oak and ash woodland with hazel, sweet chestnut and field maple coppice and an extensive network of rides. The reserve covers 294 acres (119 ha).

Birds
Sparrowhawks, tawny owls, nuthatches, treecreepers, the three species of British woodpecker and both marsh and willow tits are joined in summer by chiffchaffs, blackcaps, garden warblers, spotted flycatchers and nightingales. Whitethroats, lesser whitethroats and mallards nest on the ponds. Flocks of fieldfares and redwings, tits and finches occur in winter.

Other wildlife
Carpets of bluebells are enhanced by numerous cowslips and early purple orchids in spring. The rare Tintern (upright) spurge occurs plentifully in these woods whose ancient origin is indicated by wild service trees. Mammals include dormouse, fox and badger while purple hairstreak and white admiral are two of the butterflies.

Visiting
Access at all times. Visitors are asked to keep to the waymarked paths. A hide with disabled access overlooks a small pond.

Facilities

Warden
c/o Nagshead Nature Reserve (p120)

i St Michael's Tower, The Cross, Gloucester GL1 1PD (tel: 0452 421188).

THE LODGE,
BEDFORDSHIRE

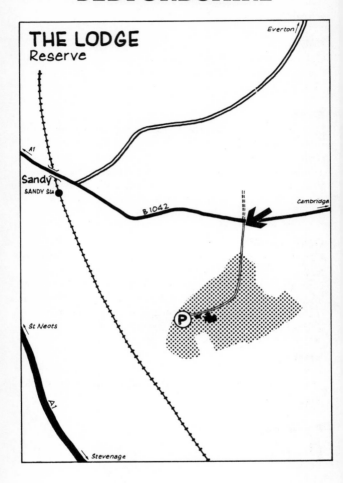

Location

The headquarters of the RSPB and its surrounding reserve is entered from the B1042 road to Potton, a mile (1.6 km) east of Sandy which is on the A1. TL/192486. The nearest railway station is in Sandy (1½ miles - 2.4 km).

The Lodge reserve is the home of the RSPB's UK headquarters and is popular with visitors. There are a number of waymarked paths around the reserve and formal gardens. There are two hides, one of which is accessible to wheelchair users. There is a shop, toilets and picnic area. Unfortunately, the house and other buildings are not open to the public.

Habitat
The reserve covers 106 acres (43 ha) of mature woodland, pine plantations, birch and bracken slopes on a ridge of Lower Greensand with a remnant of heath and an artificial lake. Formal gardens adjoin the Victorian mansion.

Birds
Green and great spotted woodpeckers, nuthatches, treecreepers, blackcaps, garden warblers, moorhens and tree pipits all breed on the reserve. Kingfishers, grey herons, sparrowhawks and crossbills are occasionally seen. Siskins and redpolls occur in winter.

Other wildlife
Muntjac deer are often seen. Several species of dragonflies frequent the lake in summer. There is a breeding colony of natterjack toads.

Visiting
The reserve and formal gardens are open daily from 9 am to 9 pm or sunset when earlier. The shop and reception is open all year 9 am to 5 pm weekdays; 10 am to 5 pm weekends.

Facilities
P   £   WC   IC   &   G   S   ☕

Warden
Mel Kemp, RSPB, The Lodge, Sandy, Bedfordshire SG19 2DL.

i 10 St Paul's Square, Bedford (tel: 0234 215226).

NAGSHEAD,
GLOUCESTERSHIRE

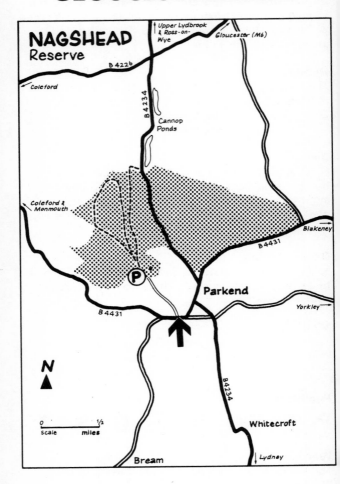

Location

Forming part of the ancient Forest of Dean, this reserve is situated immediately west of Parkend village and is signposted off the B4431 road to Coleford. SO/612078. The nearest railway station is in Lydney (6 miles - 10 km).

Two waymarked paths take visitors through this ancient oak wood. There are two hides, a seasonally staffed information centre and picnic site. It is an ideal reserve to discover woodland wildlife.

Habitat

Mature oakwood with beech, birch, rowan and holly and containing a rocky stream with a pool and clumps of alder and firs covering 761 acres (308 ha).

Birds

A large number of pied flycatchers nest mainly in boxes, as do some of the redstarts, great and blue tits and nuthatches. Other breeding species include wood warbler, chiffchaff, tree pipit, blackcap, garden warbler, treecreeper and the three species of British woodpecker. Sparrowhawks, crossbills and hawfinches are seen regularly.

Other wildlife

Bluebells and foxgloves are abundant. Silver-washed and pearl-bordered fritillaries and white admiral butterflies occur, as do dormice and fallow deer.

Visiting

Access at all times from the reserve car park and picnic area. Visitors are asked to keep to the waymarked paths of 1 mile (1.6 km) and 2 miles (3.2 km) in length. There are two hides overlooking glades and a pool. The information centre is open at weekends mid-April to August.

Facilities

P IC G s

Warden

Ivan Proctor, The Puffins, Parkend, Lydney, Gloucestershire GL15 4JA.

i St Michael's Tower, The Cross, Gloucestershire GL1 1PD (tel: 0452 421188).

RYE HOUSE MARSH,

HERTFORDSHIRE

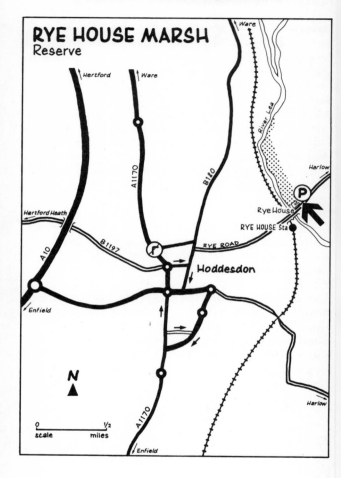

Location

In the Lee Valley Regional Park 20 miles (32 km) from central London and 300 yards (275 m) from Rye House (British Rail) station. By road turn off the A10 at Hoddesdon and follow signs for Rye Park into Rye Road. The car park is on the left after the river and railway.

This small reserve in the Lea Valley is ideal for family visits. It is served by firm paths, hides and an information centre. A wide range of events for schools and colleges is undertaken at the reserve.

Habitat
A 13 acre (6 ha) riverside marsh containing a variety of habitats including flood meadows, shallow pools and mud, fen, stands of reed and reed sweet-grass, willow and alder scrub and wet woodland.

Birds
Mallards, tufted ducks, coots, moorhens, cuckoos, reed and sedge warblers breed regularly and common terns nest on rafts on the adjacent lakes. Green and common sandpipers, many swallows and martins, warblers and yellow wagtails occur on migration. Many snipe and teals are present in winter when kingfishers, water rails, jack snipes, siskins and occasionally bitterns and bearded tits may be seen. Meadow pipits, yellowhammers and corn buntings roost on the marsh in winter.

Other wildlife
Pink water speedwell, fen bedstraw and ragged robin are among the plants. Water vole, harvest mouse and grass snake are present.

Visiting
The reserve is open daily. There are five hides and good paths and boardwalks. Two hides are accessible to wheelchairs. Rye House Marsh is primarily an RSPB Education Development Centre and specialises in field-teaching for schools, colleges and universities - details of the education programme are available from the warden.

Facilities

P £ WC IC ♿ **s**

Warden
Kevin Roberts, RSPB Rye House Marsh Reserve, Rye House, Rye Road, Hoddesdon, Hertfordshire EN11 0EJ. (tel: 0992 460031).

i The Castle, Hertford SG14 1HR (tel: 0992 584322).

SANDWELL VALLEY,
BIRMINGHAM

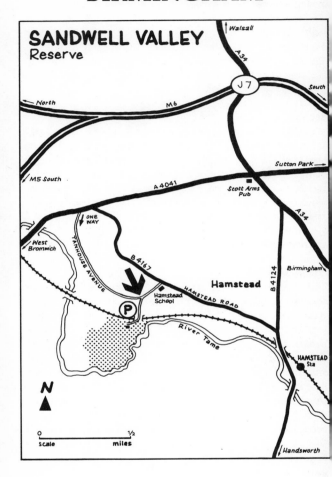

Location

Forming part of the Sandwell Valley Country Park in the heart of the West Midlands, the reserve is entered off Tanhouse Avenue which is reached via Hamstead Road in Great Barr. SP/036931. The nearest railway station is Hamstead (1 mile - 1.6 km).

Just a few miles from the centre of Birmingham, this reserve is suitable for all the family. There are firm paths and hides overlooking the marsh and lake. The reserve has an information centre serving limited refreshments and is an Education Development Centre.

Habitat
This is a diverse urban reserve covering 25 acres (10 ha), consisting of lake, marsh and reclaimed grassland.

Birds
Mallards, tufted ducks, coots, moorhens, little ringed plovers, lapwings, snipe, reed, sedge and willow warblers, whitethroats and willow tits all breed. Common terns and great crested grebes occur in the summer. Curlews, dunlins, green and common sandpipers and greenshanks visit on migration. Wigeons and pochards frequent the lake in winter, with teals in the marsh where snipe, jack snipe and water rails may be seen.

Other wildlife
Many species of butterflies are seen each year. Chicory and coltsfoot flower on the higher ground.

Visiting
Access at all times to the car park from where firm paths lead to four hides overlooking the marsh, lake and wader scrape. The information centre, with shop and toilets, is open 9 am to 5 pm (Monday - Thursday), 10 am to 5 pm (Saturday and Sunday), closed Friday, and provides a panoramic view of the reserve. School parties from primary to sixth-form level are welcome by appointment.

Facilities

P   WC   IC   &   G   s   ☕

Warden
Tony Whitehead, RSPB Nature Centre, 20 Tanhouse Avenue, Great Barr B43 5AG (tel: 021 358 3013).

i Convention and Visitor Bureau, 2 City Arcade, Birmingham B2 4TX (tel: 021 643 2514).

DEFENDER, DISCOVERY, RANGE ROVER, THE BEST 4x4'sxFAR.

LAND ROVER. LODE LANE. SOLIHULL. ENGLAND B92 8NW.

CHURNET VALLEY WOODS,

STAFFORDSHIRE

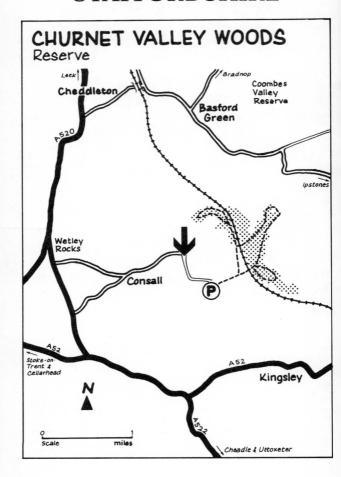

Location

Lying in the steep-sided valley of the River Churnet, the three properties of Chase Wood, Rough Knipe and Booths Wood are entered down the minor road from Consall village, east of the A522 from Cheadle to Leek. SS/990489. The nearest railway station is Stoke-on-Trent (13 miles - 21 km).

The circular woodland walks are reached by foot from the nearby Country Park car park. Stout footwear is advisable at all times.

Habitat
Mature broadleaved woodland clothing the valley slopes rises to 200 ft (60 m) above the river and canal and contains oak, ash, wych elm, rowan, bird cherry, guelder rose and hazel. The reserve covers 183 acres (74 ha).

Birds
The resident species of nuthatch, treecreeper, sparrowhawk, tits and woodpeckers are joined in summer by numerous garden warblers, blackcaps, willow warblers, wood warblers and redstarts with several pairs of whitethroats, lesser whitethroats and pied flycatchers. Siskins and redpolls occur in winter.

Other wildlife
Giant bellflower, broadleaved helleborine and wild garlic flower in the woodland where white-letter hairstreak butterflies may be seen. Grass snakes are common.

Visiting
Access at all times on foot from the Country Park car park off the private road (SJ/995483). Visitors should walk downhill to the canal bridge where waymarked paths enter the three woods for circular walks.

Facilities
P

Warden
Maurice Waterhouse, Coombes Valley Reserve (see page 131).

i Market Place, Leek, Staffordshire ST13 5HH (tel: 0538 381000).

COOMBES VALLEY,
STAFFORDSHIRE

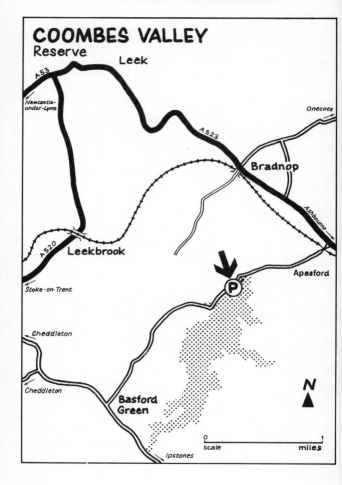

Location

This secluded valley lies off the A523 road to Ashbourne, three miles (4.8 km) south-east of Leek. Turn up the minor road to Apesford (as signposted) and the reserve is entered after one mile (1.6 km). SK/009534. The nearest railway station is Stoke-on-Trent (13 miles - 21 km).

This wooded valley reserve is served by waymarked paths, hides and an information centre. Some of the paths are steep and rugged.

Habitat
A steep-sided valley of 263 acres (106 ha) with a rocky stream and slopes covered by oak woodland, bracken clearings and pasture.

Birds
Redstarts, wood warblers and pied flycatchers are typical breeding birds and there are also tree pipits, sparrowhawks, tawny and long-eared owls and the three species of woodpeckers. Dippers, grey wagtails and kingfishers frequent the stream. Large flocks of fieldfares, redwings, tits and finches occur in winter.

Other wildlife
This is a fine site for badgers which breed in several setts. There is a rich beetle fauna. Several orchid species occur.

Visiting
Open daily except Tuesday, from 9 am to 9 pm or sunset when earlier. A nature trail with leaflet explores the reserve where there are two hides, one overlooking the stream and pond and another elevated in the tree canopy.

Facilities
P WC IC G

Warden
Maurice Waterhouse, Six Oaks Farm, Bradnop, Leek ST13 7EU.

i Market Place, Leek, Staffordshire ST13 5HH (tel: 0538 381000).

Kingfisher

FAIRBURN INGS,
WEST YORKSHIRE

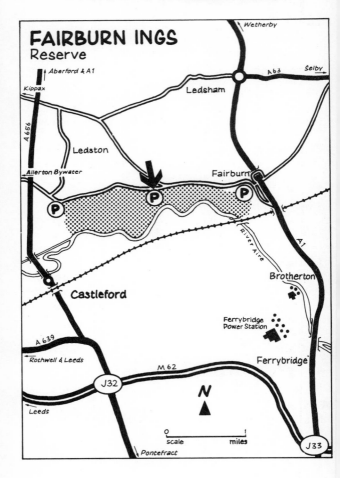

Location
Lying immediately west of the A1 north of Ferrybridge, the reserve extends along the Aire Valley from the village of Fairburn. SE/452278. The nearest railway station is in Castleford (5 miles - 8 km).

Fairburn Ings is an ideal reserve to see water birds at close quarters all year and many migrants in spring and autumn. A number of paths, some suitable for wheelchairs and pushchairs, lead to hides overlooking the lakes. There is an information centre and toilets.

Habitat
The reserve is 680 acres (243 ha) of large shallow lakes, marsh, scrub and flood-pools formed by mining subsidence; deciduous woodland by the river.

Birds
The reserve is of principal importance for wintering wildfowl including mallard, teal, shoveler, pochard, tufted duck and up to 100 whooper swans. Common, arctic and black terns, little gulls and several wader species occur on passage and both yellow and pied wagtails with swallows gather in large autumnal roosts. Lapwings, redshanks, snipe, little ringed plovers, common terns, mute swans and both great crested and little grebes nest as do several species of ducks.

Other wildlife
Interesting marshland plants and dragonflies.

Visiting
Access at all times to three public hides overlooking the lakes which are reached via the causeway and footpath below Fairburn village. The reserve information centre with toilets, a raised boardwalk through the marsh (especially suitable for wheelchairs) and a hide beside shallow pools are one mile west of the village - open at weekends and Bank holidays throughout the year from 10 am to 5 pm. Otherwise there are good views from the road lay-bys.

Facilities

P   WC   IC   ♿   G   s   ☕

Warden
Robin Horner, 2 Springholme, Caudle Hill, Fairburn, Knottingley WF11 9JQ.

i Town Hall, Wood Street, Wakefield, Yorkshire (tel: 0924 295000).

GAYTON SANDS, CHESHIRE

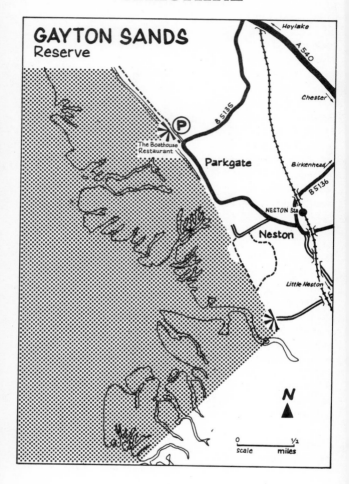

Location

Occupying a large part of the east side of the Dee Estuary, Gayton Sands is overlooked from Parkgate which is reached from the A540 Chester to Hoylake road via the B5135. SJ/274789. The nearest railway station is Neston (2 miles - 3.2 km).

Two viewpoints give good views over the estuary, which are good for birdwatching, particularly at high tides. There are no hides on the reserve.

Habitat
The reserve has extensive saltmarsh and intertidal sandflats, with a reedbed by the shore at Neston, covering 5,040 acres (2,040 ha).

Birds
Although shelducks, oystercatchers and redshanks nest on the saltmarsh, this reserve is outstanding for its large flocks of pintails, teals, mallards, wigeons and shelducks which frequent the Dee Estuary in autumn and winter. Thousands of oystercatchers, grey plovers, knots, dunlins, curlews, redshanks and bar-tailed godwits assemble on the foreshore where peregrines, merlins and hen harriers often hunt. Twites and bramblings often occur.

Other wildlife
Many moth species occur and noctule bats sometimes hunt over the edge of the saltmarsh.

Visiting
Good birdwatching, especially at high tides (times are available from the warden), can be obtained from the Old Baths car park and the adjacent public footpath, located near The Boathouse Restaurant (SJ/274789). Visitors are advised not to venture onto the saltmarsh because of very dangerous tides.

Facilities
P

Warden
Colin Wells, Burton Point Farm, Station Road, Burton, South Wirral L64 5SB.

i Town Hall, Northgate Street, Chester, Cheshire CH1 2HU (tel: 0244 317962).

In spring The Lodge reserve woodlands, home to the great spotted woodpecker, are carpeted with bluebells.

Ynys-hir in Wales is an excellent place to enjoy woodland wildli

Kestrels are common birds of prey on many RSPB nature reserves and elsewhere in the countryside.

W S Paton (RSPB)

Otters can be seen on reserves such as Coll, Islay and Leighton Moss.

G Harris (RSPB)

Birdwatching on an RSPB nature reserve is a great way to enjoy the countryside.

Ramsey Island Nature Reserve (left).

Puffins breed on several RSPB nature reserves.

Upperton's Barn at Pulborough Brooks, has been converted into an excellent centre for visitors. The yellowhammer is just one of the birds on the reserve.

Reserves can be enjoyed at any time of the year. In the winter, Vane Farm is home to pink-footed geese.

C Carver (RSPB)

Arne Reserve in Dorset is one of the few remaining areas of heathland in southern England; it is home to the rare Dartford warbler.

Whooper swans find refuge every winter at the Lough Foyle reserve in Northern Ireland.

The RSPB and Barclays Bank are working in partnership for bird conservation.

RSPB nature reserves are not only important for birds.
At Strumpshaw Fen in the Norfolk Broads, the rare swallowtail
butterfly breeds.

Visitors can enjoy spectacular views of breeding gannets at Bempton Cliffs.

E Wright (RSPB)

Thousands of wading birds, such as oystercatchers and dunlins, gather to roost at Snettisham during the winter.

Oystercatchers are a familiar sight during the summer at Balranald, and the reserves of Orkney and Shetland.

Redshanks and other wading birds breed on wetland reserves such as West Sedgemoor, Elmley Marshes and the Ouse Washes.

Enjoy a free day out in the
English countryside
with the RSPB

We invite you to discover a
wealth of wildlife at
Leighton Moss, Minsmere
or Pulborough Brooks
RSPB nature reserve.

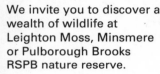

Ask one of our reserve staff
to sign this voucher to
receive free entry to one of
the RSPB's premiere nature
reserves in England.

Free entry for RSPB
members. If you are
already a member, why not
take a friend along free?

**Reserve staff, please admit
one visitor free of charge.**

Reserve staff signature.

Regd charity no 207076   49/500/93

LEIGHTON MOSS,
LANCASHIRE

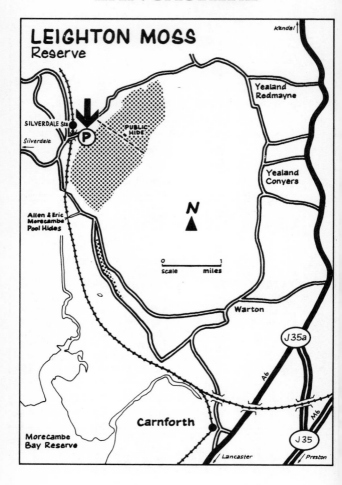

Location

Lying in a limestone valley close to the shore of Morecambe Bay, the reserve is entered close to Silverdale station and is reached from the A6(T) through Carnforth, Yealand Conyers or Yealand Redmayne. SD/478751. Silverdale railway station is next to the reserve.

This is one of the RSPB's most popular nature reserves. It is one of the few places in Britain where the rare bittern breeds. Otters also breed and are seen regularly. There is a full-range of facilities with five hides, a visitor centre with shop and tearoom, making it very suitable for a family visit. Four hides have wheelchair access.

Habitat

A large reedswamp with meres and willow and alder scrub in a valley, with woodland on its limestone slopes. The reserve covers 321 acres (130 ha).

Birds

Britain's largest concentrations of up to five pairs of bitterns breed here, together with bearded tits, reed, sedge and grasshopper warblers, teals, shovelers, pochards, tufted ducks and marsh harriers. Black terns and ospreys regularly pass through in spring and greenshanks and various sandpipers in autumn. Wintering wildfowl include large flocks of mallards, teals, wigeons, pintails and shovelers. Thousands of starlings, swallows and wagtails roost seasonally in the reeds, often attracting hunting sparrowhawks and hen harriers.

Other wildlife

Otters are resident and are frequently seen from the hides, as are roe and red deer.

Visiting

The reserve is open every day 9 am to 9 pm or sunset when earlier. Five hides overlooking various meres are linked by paths through the reeds. One is on the public causeway and is open, free of charge, at all times. The visitor centre contains interpretative displays, a tearoom and toilets. The RSPB shop is open daily 10 am to 5 pm.

Facilities

P £ WC IC ♿ G S ¶

Warden

John Wilson, Myers Farm, Silverdale, Carnforth LA5 0SW (tel: 0524 701601).

i Station Buildings, Central Promenade, Morecambe LA4 4DB (tel: 0524 582808).

Bittern

MORECAMBE BAY,

LANCASHIRE

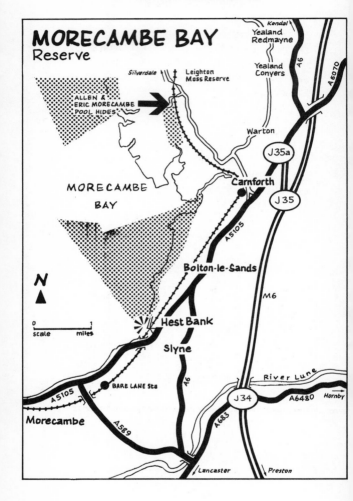

Location

The eastern side of this vast estuary may be viewed from several vantage points, notably the car park across the level-crossing at Hest Bank off the A5105 Morecambe to Carnforth road (SD/468666). A small car park off the Carnforth to Silverdale road near Leighton Moss Reserve (see page 160) provides access to hides overlooking large pools on the Carnforth saltings. SD/476737. The nearest railway station is in Silverdale (1 mile - 1.6 km).

Morecambe Bay is adjacent to the Leighton Moss Reserve. A viewpoint gives excellent views of large flocks of roosting waders and waterfowl. Two hides overlook saltmarsh pools. A visit can easily be combined with a trip to Leighton Moss.

Habitat
The reserve has extensive sheep-grazed saltmarsh and intertidal sandflats with some artificial brackish water pools on the inner side covering 3,750 acres (1.518 ha).

Birds
Of outstanding importance for its very large flocks of knots, dunlins, oystercatchers, curlews, bar-tailed godwits and redshanks which congregate, according to the tides, during most of the year except mid-summer. Sanderlings occur on May migration. Peregrines frequently hunt the waders in winter when shelducks, pintails, wigeons, red-breasted mergansers and greylag geese are present. Oystercatchers, redshanks and lapwings nest on the saltings.

Other wildlife
Bloody cranesbill, rock-rose and rock samphire flower on the limestone cliffs behind the marsh at Silverdale.

Visiting
Access to Hest Bank and the Carnforth Marsh pool hides at all times. Tide times are available from Leighton Moss Reserve. Please be aware of dangerous channels and quicksands on the foreshore.

Facilities
P (Hest Bank)

Warden
John Wilson, c/o Leighton Moss Reserve (see page 163).

i Station Buildings, Central Promenade, Morecambe LA4 4DB (tel: 0524 582808).

BEMPTON CLIFFS,
HUMBERSIDE

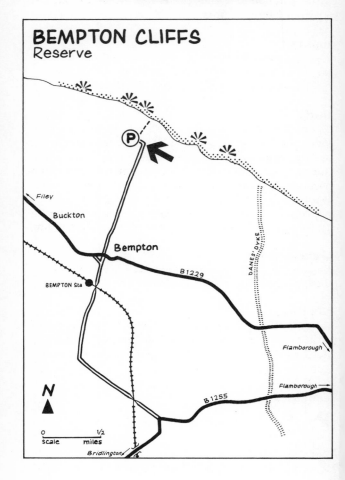

Location
Part of the spectacular chalk cliffs that stretch from
Flamborough Head to Speeton, the reserve is approached
up the cliff road from Bempton village which is on the
B1229 from Flamborough, near Bridlington, to Filey.
TA/197738. The nearest railway station is in Bempton
(1¹/2 miles - 2.4 km).

This is one of the best sites in England to see thousands of nesting seabirds including gannets and puffins at close quarters. Viewpoints overlook the cliffs, which are best visited from April to July. The seasonal visitor centre has a shop and toilets and serves light refreshments.

Habitat
Over two miles (3.6 km) of chalk cliffs with numerous cracks and ledges, rising to 400 ft (122 m) in places, and topped by a clay soil with grass and scrub.

Birds
Enormous numbers of seabirds nest on the cliffs, including thousands of guillemots, razorbills, puffins, kittiwakes, fulmars, herring gulls and several pairs of shags at the boulder base. Here the only gannetry on the mainland of England is growing annually with over 1,000 pairs. Many migrants pass offshore, including terns, skuas and shearwaters, while species such as wheatear, ring ouzel, merlin and bluethroat frequent the cliff-top on migration.

Other wildlife
Greater knapweed and pyramidal orchid flower at the cliff-top. Grey seals and porpoises are sometimes seen offshore.

Visiting
Access at all times to the cliff-top path and safe observation points providing excellent views of the seabird colonies including the gannetry. Please keep to the footpath and observation points because the cliffs are dangerous. Visitor centre (tel: 0262 851179) is open 10 am - 5 pm April - September.

Facilities
P £ (car park) **IC** & **G** **S** ☕

Warden
Present from April to September, c/o The Post Office, Bempton, near Bridlington, Humberside.

i 25 Prince Street, Bridlington, Humberside YO15 2NP (tel: 0262 673474).

BLACKTOFT SANDS,
HUMBERSIDE

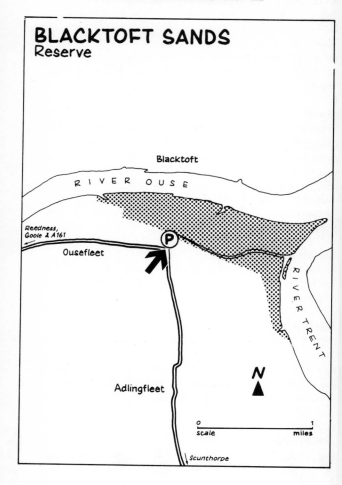

Location

Situated at the confluence of the Rivers Ouse and Trent on the inner Humber Estuary, the reserve is reached from the A161 road east of Goole through Reedness and Ousefleet. SE/843232. The nearest railway station is in Goole (8 miles - 13 km).

This large reedbed reserve is an ideal place to see a number of reedbed birds and other wildlife. Level paths lead to six hides overlooking the lagoons and reedbeds. There is an information centre and toilets.

Habitat
This 460 acre (86 ha) reserve has a large tidal reedbed, fringed by saltmarsh, with an area of shallow, brackish water lagoons.

Birds
Great crested grebes, shovelers, gadwalls, pochards and little ringed plovers nest on the lagoons which are visited by many species of waders on passage - avocet, stint, greenshank, spotted redshank, godwit, sandpiper and occasional rarities. The reedbeds contain reed and grasshopper warblers, bearded tits and water rails, and a pair of marsh harriers has occasionally nested in them. Short-eared owls, hen harriers and merlins visit in winter as do many wildfowl.

Other wildlife
Water vole, harvest mouse and fox are present.

Visiting
Open daily 9 am to 9 pm or sunset when earlier. Six hides overlook the lagoons and reeds and are approached from the car park and picnic site by firm paths.

Facilities

P £ WC IC ♿ G

Warden
Andrew Grieve, Hillcrest, High Street, Whitgift, Goole DN14 8HL.

i 75-76 Carr Lane, Hull, Humberside HU1 3RQ (tel: 0222 3559).

CAMPFIELD MARSH,
CUMBRIA

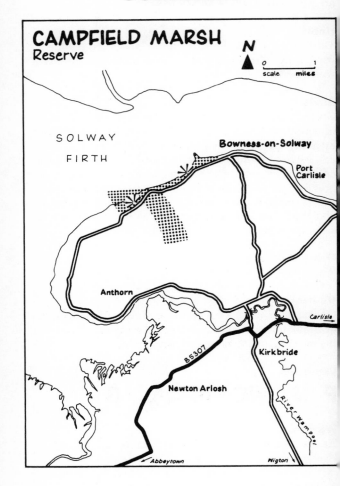

Location

Forming part of the southern shore of the Solway Estuary, Campfield Marsh is overlooked from the minor road west of Bowness-on-Solway which is reached by the B5307 road from Carlisle. NY/207620. The nearest railway station is in Carlisle (13 miles - 21 km).

The reserve can be easily viewed from lay-bys overlooking the Solway Firth giving good views of estuary birds. There are large flocks of waders and geese in the winter.

Habitat
Tidal saltmarsh with gorse scrub, grazed pasture with some areas of open water and part of Bowness Common, one of the largest lowland raised mires in the country. The reserve covers 555 acres (225 ha).

Birds
At high tide the saltmarsh supports the largest wader roosts on the estuary with oystercatchers, knots, curlews, grey plovers and bar-tailed godwits among others. Farther out on the Solway large flocks of wildfowl including wigeon and scaup occur in winter, as well as divers and grebes. Peregrines, merlins and barn owls are often seen hunting and in late winter pink-footed geese re-fuel before leaving for Iceland.

Other wildlife
The typical saltmarsh flora is enhanced by a colony of northern marsh orchid while on the mire sundew, bog rosemary and spotted orchid can be seen along with adder, large heath butterfly and roe deer.

Visiting
Good views of the high-tide roosts can be obtained from the roadside lay-bys. Please do not go onto the marsh. Escorted access to farmland and mire may be arranged by written application to the warden.

Facilities

P

Warden
Norman Holton, North Plain Farm, Bowness-on-Solway, Carlisle, Cumbria CA5 5AG.

i Old Town Hall, Green Market, Carlisle CA3 8JH (tel: 0228 512444).

HAWESWATER,
CUMBRIA

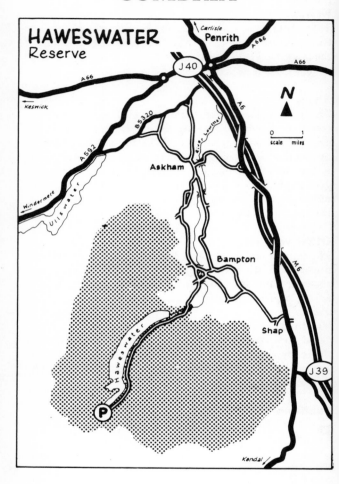

Location

Lying within the Lakeland hills, the Haweswater Valley is approached from the M6 at Shap (Junction 39) or Penrith (Junction 40) by taking the road to Bampton and following the sign to Haweswater or Mardale. A car park is situated at the southern end of the reservoir. NY/470108. The nearest railway station is in Penrith (10 miles - 16 km).

Haweswater is the only site in England where golden eagles nest. An observation point is open during the nesting season. There is free access to the remainder of the reserve. As the terrain is uneven stout footwear should be worn.

Habitat

The reserve has steep oak and birch woodland surrounded by fells with rocky streams and some heather moor covering 23,222 acres (9,395 ha).

Birds

England's only pair of golden eagles nests on high crags near the head of the reservoir. The other upland breeding birds include peregrine, raven, ring ouzel, golden plover, curlew, redshank and snipe while the woodland has pied flycatcher, wood warbler, tree pipit and redstart as well as buzzard and sparrowhawk.

Other wildlife

Bird's-eye primrose, lesser twayblade and globe flower are special plants. The woodland is rich in ferns, mosses and lichens. Red squirrels and both roe and red deer may be seen.

Visiting

Wardens run an observation post from 8 am to 6 pm April - August provided the eagles are nesting - reached by a path from the reservoir car park (NY/469108). Otherwise free access to the fells - but not in the eagles' valley during the breeding season please.

Facilities

P

Warden

John Day, 7 Naddlegate, Burn Banks, near Penrith CA10 2RL.

i Robinson's School, Middlegate, Penrith CA11 7PT (tel: 0768 7466).

HODBARROW,
CUMBRIA

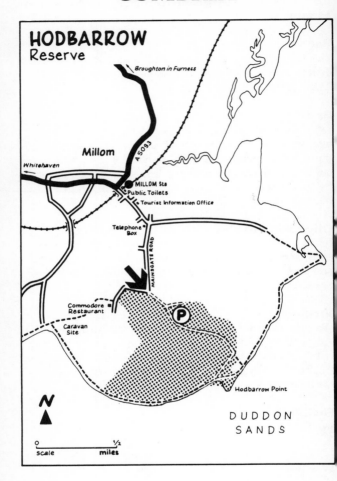

Location

Lying beside the Duddon Estuary, Hodbarrow is approached from Millom via Mainsgate Road, turning left at its end for the reserve entrance. SD/174791. The nearest railway station is in Millom (2 miles - 3.2 km).

Hodbarrow is a quiet coastal reserve, with a level path around the lagoon. A hide overlooks the tern island and wader roost.

Habitat
Slightly brackish lagoon bordered by limestone scrub and grassland and the estuary bank covering 260 acres (105 ha).

Birds
Little, common and Sandwich terns, oystercatchers and ringed plovers nest on the sea bank. Many migrants including warblers frequent the scrub. Hundreds of wigeons, teals, mallards, goldeneyes, red-breasted mergansers and coots winter on the lagoon whose shores are used by oystercatchers, redshanks and dunlins for roosting during high winter tides. There is a herd of over 50 mute swans.

Other wildlife
The rare natterjack toad breeds in shallow pools. Bloody cranesbill and several orchid species flower in the grassland.

Visiting
Access at all times from the informal car parks along a footpath around the lagoon including the exposed seawall, with views also over the estuary.

Facilities
P

Warden
c/o RSPB North of England Office (page 295).

i Millom Folk Museum, St George's Road, Millom LA18 4DQ (tel: 0229 772555).

Sandwich tern

ST BEES HEAD,
CUMBRIA

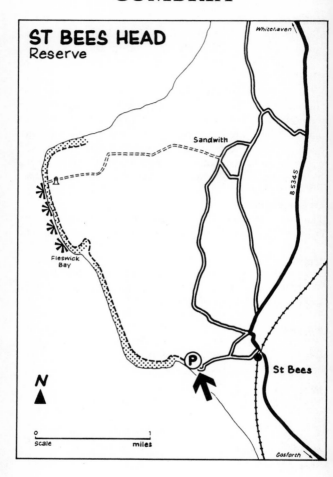

Location

This cliff headland lies south of Whitehaven and west of the B5345 road to St Bees. NX/962118. The nearest railway station is in St Bees (1/2 mile - 1 km).

Four viewpoints overlook this cliff seabird colony reached by a public footpath from the car park, which has a toilet. The walk to the viewpoint is long and steep in parts.

Habitat

Three miles (4.8 km) of sandstone cliffs, up to 300 ft (90 m) high, with many ledges and grassy tops with gorse patches.

Birds

The reserve holds the largest cliff seabird colony on the west coast of England containing razorbills, guillemots, kittiwakes, herring gulls, fulmars, a small number of puffins and the only black guillemots breeding in England. Rock pipits, ravens, peregrines, stonechats, whitethroats, shags and cormorants also frequent the cliffs. Gannets, skuas, terns, shearwaters and eiders may be seen offshore at various times.

Other wildlife

Rock samphire, bloody cranesbill and heath spotted orchid flower on the cliff-top.

Visiting

A public footpath from the public car park (NX/962118) on St Bees beach goes north along the cliffs to four viewing points. Cars with disabled visitors may use the private road to the lighthouse from Sandwith - otherwise no access. Visitors should not attempt to reach the beach between the north and south headlands other than at Fleswick Bay.

Facilities

P WC

Warden

c/o RSPB North of England Office (page 295).

i Market Hall, Market Place, Whitehaven, Cumbria CA28 7JG (tel: 0946 695678).

Scotland

Greenshank

BARON'S HAUGH,
STRATHCLYDE

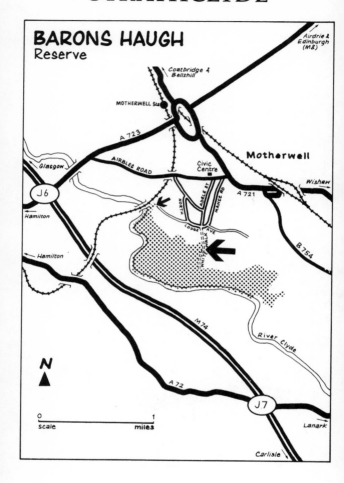

Location

Lying in the Clyde Valley one mile (1.6 km) south of Motherwell town centre, the reserve is signposted via Adele Street opposite Motherwell Civic Centre then by a lane leading off North Lodge Avenue. NS/755552. The nearest railway station is in Motherwell (1/2 mile - 1 km).

This marshland reserve is one mile from Motherwell. Four hides overlook the marsh with a two-hour circular walk.

Habitat

Marsh (the haugh) with permanently flooded areas, woodland, scrub, meadows and parkland beside the River Clyde. The reserve covers 265 acres (107 ha).

Birds

The haugh attracts wigeons, teals, mallards, pochards and tufted ducks in winter as well as over 50 whooper swans. Little grebes, redshanks, sedge and grasshopper warblers nest here with kingfishers and common sandpipers along the river. Other breeding birds include garden warblers, whinchats and sparrowhawks.

Other wildlife

Roe deer are occasionally seen.

Visiting

Access at all times. Four hides overlook the haugh (two of which are accessible to wheelchairs) and there is a two-hour walk around the reserve.

Facilities

Warden

Russell Nisbet, 9 Wisteria Lane, Carluke ML8 5TB.

i The Library, Hamilton Road, Motherwell, Strathclyde (tel: 0698 251311).

Whooper swan

COLL,

STRATHCLYDE

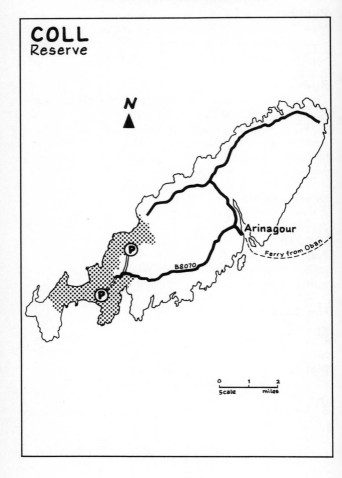

Location

The reserve is situated at the west end of the Hebridean island of Coll. Take the B8070 west from the village of Arinagour and park where the road terminates, after six miles (10 km).

Reached by ferry from Oban, this reserve is a mix of
beaches, hay meadows and moorland. It is one of Britain's
remaining sites for breeding corncrakes.

Habitat
The reserve covers 2,496 acres (1,010 ha) of beaches, sand
dunes, machair, fen meadows, hay meadows and moorland.

Birds
Coll is of principal importance for corncrakes, which nest
in the hay meadows. The machair has a high density of
breeding waders. Large flocks of barnacle and
Greenland white-fronted geese overwinter.

Other wildlife
The reserve is very rich botanically, with fine examples of
sand dune and machair flora - stunning in early summer.
Seals and otters are present.

Visiting
The sand dune and beach habitats are open all year to
walkers. To avoid disturbing corncrakes and trampling the
hay crop, please do not enter hayfields. Corncrakes are very
rarely seen and can be heard without going into the fields.

Facilities
P

Warden
Charlie Self, Totronald, Isle of Coll, Argyll PA78 7PB.

Ferries
Cross from Oban. Enquiries to Caledonian Macbrayne,
Ferry Terminal, Gourock PA19 1QP (tel: 0475 33755).

INVERSNAID,
CENTRAL

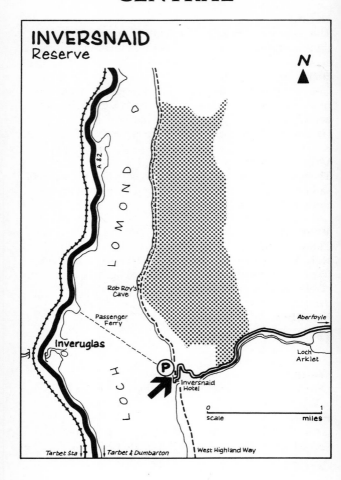

Location

Lying on the east side of Loch Lomond, this Trossachs reserve is approached by an unclassified road by taking the B829 west from Aberfoyle. NN/337088. The nearest railway station is in Stirling (35 miles - 56 km).

Set on the shores of Loch Lomond, this reserve is a mixture of woodland and moorland. A path through the wood offers a pleasant walk. The path is steep and rugged in parts and is not suitable for pushchairs.

Habitat

The ground rises steeply from Loch Lomond through deciduous woodland to a craggy ridge, beyond which lies moorland of grass and heather. Several mountain burns descend to the loch. The reserve covers 923 acres (374 ha).

Birds

The resident woodland birds are joined by summer migrants such as wood warbler, redstart, pied flycatcher and tree pipit. Buzzards nest on the crags and in the woods and blackcocks frequent the lower slopes. Dippers, grey wagtails and common sandpipers breed on the loch shore and along the burns. The loch itself is a migration route especially for wildfowl and waders.

Other wildlife

The bryophyte and lichen communities are exceptional. Badger, feral goat and both red and roe deer are present.

Visiting

Access at all times along the long-distance footpath, the West Highland Way, which follows the loch shore; nature trail offers a pleasant woodland walk. There is a car park at the road end by Inversnaid Hotel where toilets are available during the summer. A pedestrian ferry crosses from Inveruglas on the west bank of Loch Lomond, mainly in summer: telephone Inversnaid Hotel (087 786 223) for arrangements.

Facilities

P WC G

Warden

Mike Trubridge, West Garage House, Gribloch, Kippen, Stirling FK8 3HS.

i Main Street, Aberfoyle, Central (tel: 087 72 352).

KEN-DEE MARSHES,
DUMFRIES & GALLOWAY

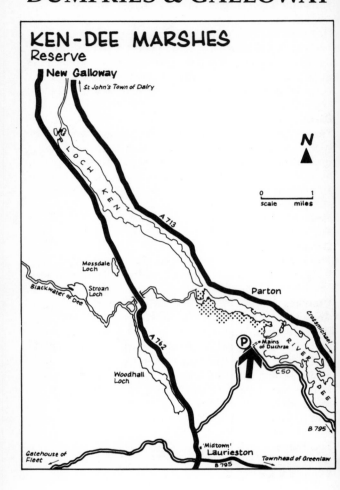

Location

Lying in the valley of the River Dee between New Galloway and Castle Douglas, the reserve occurs in several parts beside the River Dee and upstream of Loch Ken. The nearest railway station is in Dumfries (6 miles - 10 km).

A number of paths cross the reserve giving good views of the marshes and meadows.

Habitat
Marshes and meadows of the River Dee floodplain bordered by hillside farmland and deciduous woods covering 378 acres (153 ha).

Birds
In winter some 300 Greenland white-fronted geese visit the valley together with greylag geese, wigeons, pintails, teals, mallards, shovelers, goosanders and whooper swans. Hen harriers, peregrines and buzzards hunt the area. The marshland breeding birds include redshank, great crested grebe, teal and shoveler while redstart, pied flycatcher, wood warbler and willow tit nest in the woodland. Crossbills and siskins occur locally.

Other wildlife
Red squirrels, roe deer and otters are resident.

Visiting
There is general access to the reserve from the RSPB car park at the entrance to Mains of Duchrae Farm. Good views of other marshes are obtained from the minor road off the A762 to the west and A713 to the east.

Facilities
G

Warden
Ray Hawley, Midtown, Laurieston, Nr Castle Douglas, Dumfries and Galloway DG7 2PP.

i Markethill Car Park, Castle Douglas, Dumfries and Galloway (tel: 0556 2611).

Otter

LOCH GRUINART, ISLAY, STRATHCLYDE

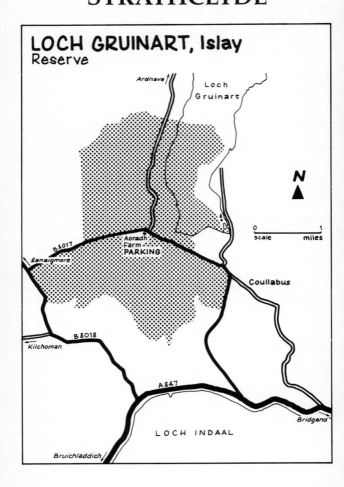

Location

Situated in the north of the Hebridean island of Islay, the reserve lies on the south and west of Loch Gruinart and straddles the B8017 road west of Bridgend.

This reserve is famous for the large numbers of geese that spend the winter here. The reserve can be seen easily from the road, letting you birdwatch from your car. There is a small visitor centre with video link to grazing geese in the winter.

Habitat
The reserve covers 4,087 acres (1,654 ha) of improved and rough pasture 'flats' with saltmarsh at the head of the tidal Loch Gruinart; also moorland with patches of woodland and hill lochs.

Birds
The major feeding and roosting site in the British Isles for the Greenland race of barnacle geese, numbering up to 20,000 when they overwinter on Islay from October to April. Also large flocks of white-fronted geese are present. Hen harriers, buzzards and short-eared owls breed and may be seen also in winter with golden eagles, peregrines, merlins, whooper swans and choughs. Teals, redshanks, snipe, curlews and stonechats nest.

Other wildlife
Otters, grey and common seals and both red and roe deer are often seen.

Visiting
Good birdwatching may be obtained from the B8017, the visitor centre and the hide beside the minor road north to Ardnave. Parking is available both here and at Aoradh Farm (NR/276673). To avoid disturbing the geese or livestock please do not enter the fields. Visitor centre is open daily (10 am - 5 pm).

Facilities

P IC ♿

Warden
Mike Peacock, Grainel, Gruinart, Bridgend, Isle of Islay PA44 7PS.

Ferries
Cross daily from Kennacraig, on Kintyre, to Port Ellen. Enquiries to Caledonian MacBrayne, Ferry Terminal, Gourock PA19 1QP (tel: 0475 33755).

Air
There is a service from Glasgow to Port Ellen. Enquiries to Loganair (tel: 041 889 3181).

LOCHWINNOCH,
STRATHCLYDE

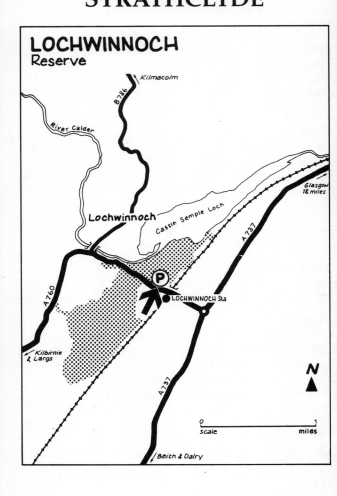

Location

The nature centre and reserve lie off the A760 road from Largs to Paisley, 1/2 mile (1 km) east of Lochwinnoch. NS/359581. Lochwinnoch station is opposite the centre.

This is an ideal family nature reserve, with trails, hides, a visitor centre and observation tower. A programme of events is carried out in the summer.

Habitat

This reserve comprises 388 acres (157 ha) of the shallow Barr Loch and the sedge marsh of Aird Meadow together with some alder and willow scrub and deciduous woodland.

Birds

A stronghold of great crested grebes breed here with snipe, shovelers, tufted ducks, black-headed gulls, grey herons, sedge and grasshopper warblers. Whimbrels and greenshanks occur on autumn passage. In winter, whooper swans, greylag geese, goosanders, wigeons, teals, pochards and goldeneyes frequent the loch. Kestrels, sparrowhawks and occasionally peregrines may be seen throughout the year.

Other wildlife

Marsh marigold, yellow water-lily, valerian and both common spotted and greater butterfly orchids flower. Roe deer are seen frequently, otters occasionally.

Visiting

The reserve is open daily from 9 am to 9 pm or sunset when earlier. The nature trails incorporate four hides overlooking the marsh and open water. The centre, with observation tower and RSPB shop, is open daily from 10 am to 5 pm. Refreshments are served at weekends.

Facilities

P £ WC IC ♿ **G S** ☕ (weekends)

Warden

Graham Christer, Lochwinnoch Nature Centre, Largs Road, Lochwinnoch, Strathclyde (tel: 0505 842663).

i Town Hall, Abbey Close, Paisley, Strathclyde (tel: 041 889 0711).

Marsh marigold

MULL OF GALLOWAY,
DUMFRIES & GALLOWAY

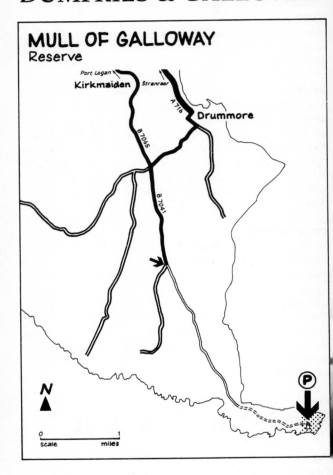

Location

Lying at the southern tip of the peninsula south of Stranraer, the reserve is reached via the A716 road to Drummore, then the minor road to the lighthouse and cliffs. NX/157304. The nearest railway station is Stranraer (21 miles - 34 km).

This small cliff reserve gives good views of nesting seabirds during the spring and summer.

Habitat
Rugged granite cliffs covering 3/4 mile (1.2 km) on the peninsula headland.

Birds
There are nesting colonies of guillemots, razorbills, kittiwakes, black guillemots, shags, cormorants, fulmars and both great black-backed and herring gulls. Manx shearwaters and gannets regularly pass the headland.

Other wildlife
Plants of the cliff-top include spring squill and purple milk vetch.

Visiting
Access at all times, but visitors are warned not to go to the cliff edge which is dangerous.

Warden
None present. Enquiries Wood of Cree Reserve (page 197).

i Port Rodie Car Park, Stranraer, Dumfries and Galloway (tel: 0776 2595).

Guillemot with young

WOOD OF CREE,

DUMFRIES & GALLOWAY

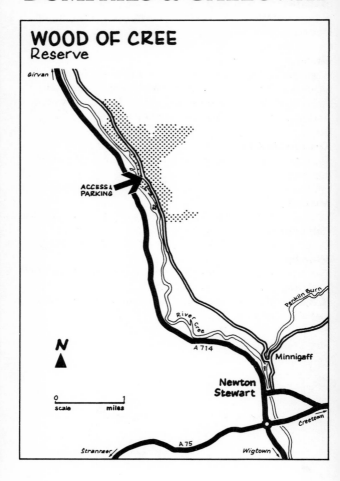

Location

Rising from the east bank of the River Cree four miles
(6.4 km) north-west of Newton Stewart, the reserve is
approached on the minor road from Minnigaff running
parallel to the A714. NX/382708. The nearest railway station
is in Barrhill (14 miles - 22 km).

This large broadleaved woodland gives visitors an excellent opportunity to explore woodland wildlife. A simple track leads visitors through the reserve from the car park.

Habitat
One of the largest broadleaved woods in the south of Scotland, consisting largely of old coppice of sessile oak, birch and hazel. Several burns tumble down through the wood from the moorland above to the riverside marsh. The reserve is 659 acres (267 ha) in size.

Birds
Redstarts, pied flycatchers, wood warblers, tree pipits, garden warblers, woodcocks, great spotted woodpeckers, buzzards and sparrowhawks breed in the woods. Common sandpipers, dippers and grey wagtails frequent the streams and mallards, teals and oystercatchers frequent the riverside.

Other wildlife
Roe deer and otters are present. Purple hairstreak and dark green fritillary are among the butterflies.

Visiting
Access at all times along a woodland track which leads up from the roadside car park.

Facilities
P G

Warden
Paul Collin, Gairland, Old Edinburgh Road, Minigaff, Newton Stewart DG8 6PL.

i Dashwood Square, Newton Stewart, Dumfries and Galloway (tel: 0671 2431).

FOWLSHEUGH,
GRAMPIAN

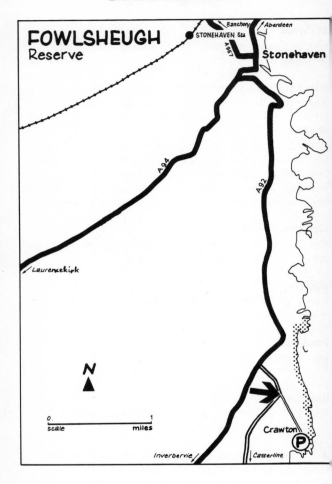

Location

The small cliff-top car park for this reserve is at Crawton which is signposted from the A92 road to Inverbervie three miles (4.8 km) south of Stonehaven. NO/876805. The nearest railway station is in Stonehaven.

This cliff-top reserve is at its best in the spring and summer when thousands of nesting seabirds can be seen at close quarters. There is a simple path along the cliff to several viewpoints.

Habitat
Old Red Sandstone grass-topped cliffs with nooks and ledges covering 1 1/2 miles (2.4 km).

Birds
There are very large colonies of guillemots, razorbills and kittiwakes with smaller numbers of fulmars, herring gulls, shags and puffins nesting on the cliffs. Eiders occur offshore.

Other wildlife
Seals and bottle-nosed dolphins are seen occasionally.

Visiting
Access at all times along the cliff-top path from which the seabirds may be viewed well at several points. Visitors are warned to take care at the cliff-edge.

Facilities
P

Warden
Present in summer. Enquiries to RSPB East Scotland Office (page 295).

 66 Allardice Street, Stonehaven, Grampian (tel: 0569 62806).

Eiders

KILLIECRANKIE,
TAYSIDE

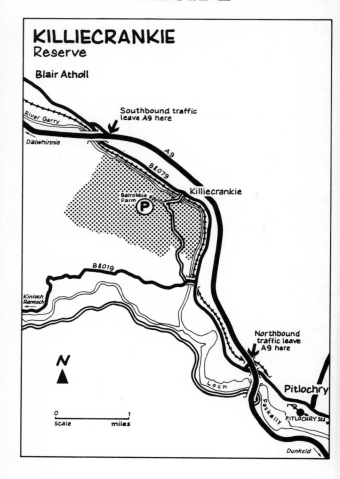

Location

Lying in Highlands scenery, this reserve is reached by
turning off the main A9 road just north of Pitlochry and
proceeding to Killicrankie on the B8079 road, then taking
the minor road south-westwards to the warden's house at
NN/907627. The nearest railway station is in Pitlochry
(4 miles - 6.4 km).

A number of waymarked trails lead visitors through the mixed oakwoods to heather moorland.

Habitat
Sessile oakwoods also containing birch, ash, wych elm and alder rise from the gorge of the River Garry to a plateau of pastureland. Above this a birchwood ascends steeply through crags to a ridge of heather moorland. The reserve covers 1,320 acres (534 ha).

Birds
Wood warblers, redstarts, tree pipits and pied flycatchers nest in the woodland, as well as garden warblers, crossbills, sparrowhawks, buzzards and both green and great spotted woodpeckers. Black grouse and whinchats frequent the moorland fringe; kestrels, and sometimes ravens, inhabit the crags. Both golden eagles and peregrines are seen occasionally.

Other wildlife
Red squirrels and roe deer are plentiful. A rich reserve flora includes yellow mountain saxifrage, globe flower, grass of Parnassus and several species of orchids.

Visiting
Access to the waymarked trails at all times. Visitors may be escorted by written arrangement with the warden.

Facilities
P   G

Warden
Martin Robinson, Balrobbie Farm, Killiecrankie, Pitlochry PH16 5LJ.

i 22 Atholl Road, Pitlochry, Tayside (tel: 0796 472215).

LOCH OF KINNORDY,
TAYSIDE

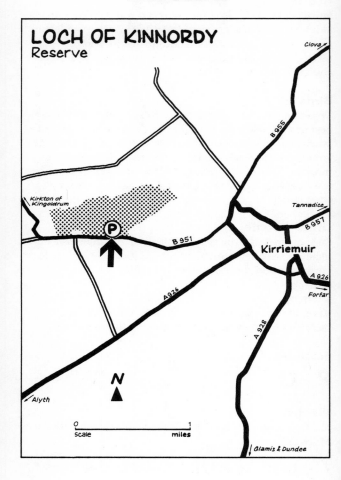

Location

Situated off the B951 road one mile (1.6 km) west of Kirriemuir. NO/361539. The nearest railway station is in Dundee (18 miles - 29 km).

During the summer it is possible to see ospreys fishing in the loch on this reserve. There are a number of simple paths leading to hides overlooking the loch and marsh.

Habitat
A freshwater marsh with varying amounts of open water, containing willow and alder scrub, fringed by woodland and set in a farming landscape. The reserve is 200 acres (81 ha) in size.

Birds
Mallards, teals, shovelers, tufted ducks, gadwalls, great crested and little grebes nest as well as sedge warblers, reed buntings, redshanks and a large colony of black-headed gulls. Up to six pairs of black-necked grebes have bred here recently. Sparrowhawks and long-eared owls occur and ospreys and marsh harriers feed regularly at the loch in the summer. A large roost of pink-footed geese gathers in winter with a variety of ducks and hunting short-eared owls.

Other wildlife
The rich flora includes cowbane, greater spearwort and northern marsh orchid. Red squirrels are present and otters have occurred.

Visiting
Open 9 am to sunset daily, apart from Saturdays in September, October and November. Paths lead from a small car park to the hides.

Facilities
P

Warden
A warden is present from April to August at The Flat, Kinnordy Home Farm, Kirriemuir DD8 5ER. Enquiries at other times to Killiecrankie Reserve (page 201).

i High Street, Kirriemuir, Tayside (tel: 0575 74097).

LOCH OF STRATHBEG, GRAMPIAN

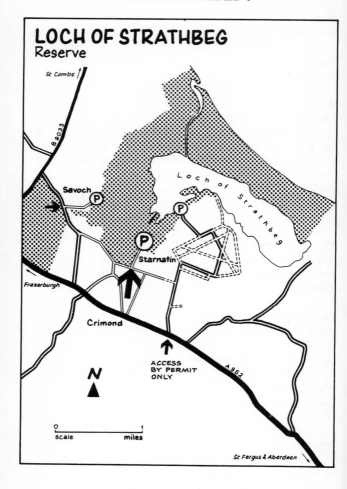

Location

Lying between the sea and the A952 Peterhead to Fraserburgh road near the village of Crimond. NK/063564. The nearest railway station is Aberdeen (40 miles - 64 km).

The visitor centre on this reserve overlooks the Loch giving good views of wading birds and waterfowl, particularly during the winter. There are also a number of trails, one of which is suitable for wheelchair users.

Habitat

A large shallow loch on the Aberdeenshire coast, separated from the sea by wide sand dunes and bordered by freshwater fen and marsh, saltmarsh, woodland and farmland. The reserve covers 2,592 acres (1,049 ha).

Birds

Large numbers of whooper swans and pink-footed geese gather on and around the loch which also serves as a migration staging post. There are also tufted ducks, pochards, goldeneyes, red-breasted mergansers, goosanders, wigeons, mallards and teals. From the observation room, in addition to the wildfowl, a good number of waders can be seen, especially during the migration seasons. These include greenshanks, green and wood sandpipers, ruffs and black-tailed godwits. Breeding birds include Sandwich terns, water rails, sedge and willow warblers.

Other wildlife

Roe deer and otters are seen frequently. Badgers are also present. Lesser butterfly orchids and coral-root orchids also occur.

Visiting

The reserve and visitor centre are open at all times. Hides overlook the loch and other parts of the reserve. There is also a boardwalk through the fen woodland.

Facilities

P IC

Warden

Jim Dunbar, The Lythe, Crimongate, Lonmay, Fraserburgh, Grampian AB43 4UB.

i Saltoun Square, Fraserburgh, Grampian (tel: 0346 518315).

VANE FARM,
TAYSIDE

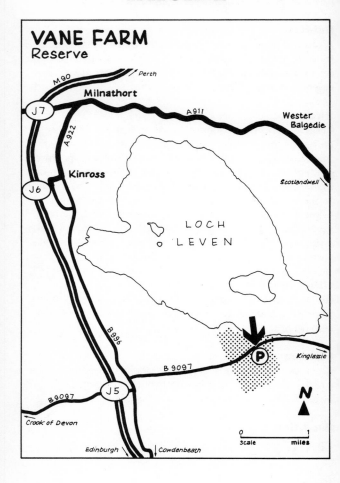

Location

Lying on the southern shore of Loch Leven east of Kinross, the reserve and nature centre are entered off the B9097 road to Glenrothes two miles (3.2 km) east of junction 5 on the M90. NT/160991. The nearest railway station is Cowdenbeath (8 miles - 13 km).

This is one of the most popular RSPB reserves in Scotland. The visitor centre with shop, toilets and weekend refreshments overlooks Loch Leven. A trail leads visitors to a hide on the Loch shore.

Habitat

A variety of habitats surround this educational nature centre, which overlooks Loch Leven, including open water, wet and dry grassland, birch and mixed woodland and heather moorland with rocky outcrops. The reserve covers 569 acres (230 ha).

Birds

The reserve is renowned for pink-footed geese, with up to 23,000 arriving in autumn. Whooper swans, greylag geese, wigeons, teals, mallards and pintails also visit during the winter. The woodlands have both tawny and long-eared owls, green and great spotted woodpeckers, tree pipits, spotted flycatchers and willow warblers. Great crested and little grebes, shelducks, gadwalls, shovelers and tufted ducks nest by lagoons and the wet grassland areas provide nesting habitat for lapwings, oystercatchers, curlews, snipe and redshanks.

Other wildlife

Over 250 species of plants have been recorded. Roe deer and fox are regularly seen.

Visiting

Access at all times to the car park and nature trail. A hide overlooks the scrape. The nature centre with observation room and RSPB shop is open daily from April to Christmas, 10 am to 5 pm, but from 10 am to 4 pm January to March. School parties and groups are especially welcome by appointment.

Facilities

P £ WC IC & G S ☕(weekends)

Warden

David Fairlamb, Vane Farm Nature Centre, Kinross KY13 7LX (tel: 0577 862355).

i Kinross Service Area, Junction 6, M90, Kinross, Tayside (tel: 0577 863680).

Enjoy a free day out in
Scotland with the RSPB

We invite you to discover a wealth of wildlife at Loch Garten, Vane Farm or Lochwinnoch RSPB nature reserve.

Ask one of our reserve staff to sign this voucher to receive free entry to one of the RSPB's premiere Scottish nature reserves.

Free entry for RSPB members. If you are already a member, why not take a friend along free?

Reserve staff, please admit one visitor free of charge.

Reserve staff signature

Regd charity no 207076   49/500/93

ABERNETHY FOREST,
HIGHLAND

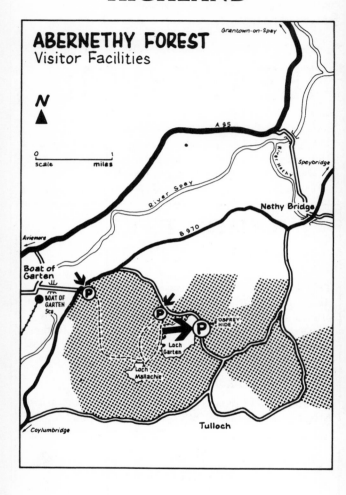

Location

Renowned for its osprey centre, overlooking the site where the ospreys returned to breed in 1959, this Strathspey reserve comprises a large portion of Abernethy Forest south of the villages of Boat of Garten and Nethybridge. Loch Garten is signposted from the B970 linking the two villages. NH/978184. The nearest BR station is Aviemore (9 miles - 14 km).

Abernethy Forest reserve incorporates the famous Loch Garten osprey site. Ospreys have nested here since 1959 and a well equipped observation centre overlooks the nest site. There are several nature trails, some of which are suitable for wheelchairs and pushchairs. Unfortunately, we are unable to provide toilet facilities; the nearest public toilets are in Boat of Garten, four miles away. Due to the fragile habitat and rare wildlife found on the reserve, visitor facilities are only available at Loch Garten.

Habitat
The reserve holds one of the most important remnants of the once extensive Scots pine forest of the Scottish Highlands. It also contains forest bogs, moorland, mountain top, lochs and crofting land. The reserve covers 30,760 acres (12,450 ha).

Birds
In addition to the regular nesting pair of ospreys, crested tits, Scottish crossbills, capercaillies, black grouse and sparrowhawks with teals, goldeneyes and wigeons on the lochs, all breed. Greylag geese, goosanders and several species of gulls roost at Loch Garten in the winter.

Other wildlife
The pinewood plants of chickweed wintergreen, bilberry and creeping lady's tresses occur. Mammals include red squirrel, pine marten, wildcat and both red and roe deer.

Visiting
The osprey centre and RSPB shop is open daily from mid-April to end August from 10 am to 8 pm. The ospreys can be viewed through binoculars and telescopes. The reserve is accessible at all times but please keep to the established tracks and paths. Waymarked woodland walks of various lengths can be followed from the two car parks. As there is a high fire risk, please do not light fires.

Facilities
P IC & G S

Warden
Forest Lodge, Nethybridge, Inverness-shire PH25 3EF.

i Grampian Road, Aviemore PH22 1PT (tel: 0479 810363). Also tourist information boards in Boat of Garten and Nethybridge.

Crested tit

BALRANALD,
WESTERN ISLES

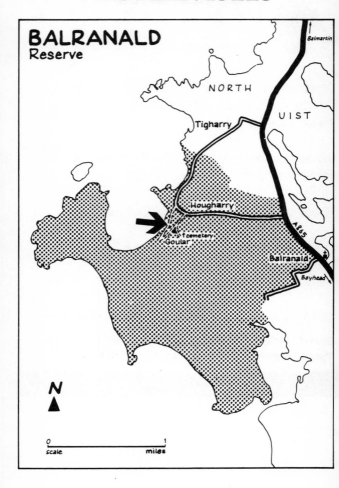

Location

Situated on the Hebridean island of North Uist, the reserve is reached by turning for Hougharry off the A865 road three miles (4.8 km) north of Bayhead. The visitor reception cottage is at Goular. NF/706707.

Set on the west coast of North Uist, this reserve is reached by ferry from Skye. The small information centre explains the importance of traditional crofting agriculture for the now rare corncrake. A simple path leads visitors around the reserve.

Habitat
Sandy, rocky beaches and dunes protect the machair from the sea. Beyond the machair lie large tracts of marshland and loch. The reserve covers 1,625 acres (658 ha).

Birds
The reserve is one of the last British strongholds of the corncrake. Lapwings, snipe, oystercatchers, ringed plovers and dunlins nest on the machair while shovelers, little grebes and tufted ducks nest in the marshes. Whooper swans, greylag geese and several birds of prey visit in winter and there is a considerable passage of birds in spring and autumn.

Other wildlife
Otters breed and are commonly seen in the freshwater lochs. Grey seals breed on the offshore island of Causamul.

Visiting
Access at all times. Visitors are asked to keep to the waymarked paths to avoid disturbing ground-nesting birds.

Facilities
IC G

Warden
Present from April to August at Goular, near Hougharry, Lochmaddy, North Uist.

i Lochmaddy, Pier Road, Isle of North Uist, Western Isles (tel: 087 63 321).

Ferries
Travel daily from Uig on Skye to Lochmaddy or from Oban to Lochboisdale on South Uist. Enquiries to Caledonian MacBrayne, Ferry Terminal, Gourock PA19 1QP (tel: 0475 33755).

Air
Nearby Benbecular is reached by air from Glasgow: enquiries to British Airways (tel: 041 332 9666).

CULBIN SANDS,

HIGHLAND / GRAMPIAN

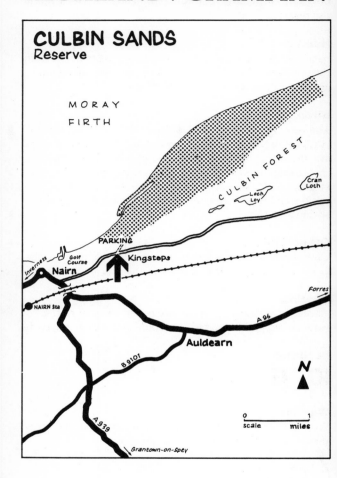

Location

On the southern shore of the Moray Firth, this reserve is entered at Kingsteps one mile (1.6 km) east of Nairn along the minor road past the golf course. NH/901573. The nearest railway station is in Nairn (1 1/2 miles - 2.4 km).

Overlooking the Moray Firth, this is a large, but little known Scottish reserve. Visitors have access to the beach at all times allowing birdwatching throughout the year, but particularly from autumn to spring.

Habitat
A long stretch of foreshore comprising sandflats, saltmarsh, shingle bars and spits, backed by the largest sand dune system in Britain, which is almost entirely afforested covering 2,822 acres (1,142 ha).

Birds
Winter flocks of bar-tailed godwits, oystercatchers, knots, dunlins, ringed plovers, redshanks and curlews with mallards, shelducks, red-breasted mergansers, greylag geese and snow buntings. Large concentrations of both common and velvet scoters with long-tailed ducks congregate offshore. Breeding birds include oystercatchers, ringed plovers and occasionally terns.

Visiting
Access at all times to the beach. Visitors should beware of the tides and creeks.

Warden
None present. Enquiries to RSPB North Scotland Office (page 295).

i 62 King Street, Nairn, Highland (tel: 0667 52753).

Dunlins

FAIRY GLEN,

HIGHLAND

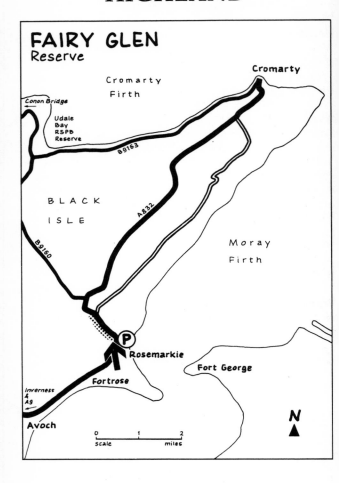

Location

On the Black Isle, Fairy Glen is entered from the car park on the northern edge of Rosemarkie just off the A832. The nearest railway station is in Inverness (15 miles - 24 km).

This small reserve allows visitors to walk through the Glen surrounded by a steep-sided wooded valley. As the path is rough in places suitable footwear is advisable.

Habitat

Six acres (2.4 ha) of broadleaved woodland in a steep-sided valley. Rosemarkie burn flows through the glen with waterfalls and a millpond.

Birds

Great spotted woodpeckers and treecreepers inhabit the wood and buzzards nest in the tree tops. Dippers and grey wagtails are frequently seen along the burn.

Visiting

Access at all times from the car park. A footpath meanders through the middle of the Glen.

Facilities

P

Warden

None present. Enquiries to RSPB North Scotland Office (page 295).

i Castle Wynd, Inverness (tel: 0463 234353).

Dipper

GLENBORRODALE,
HIGHLAND

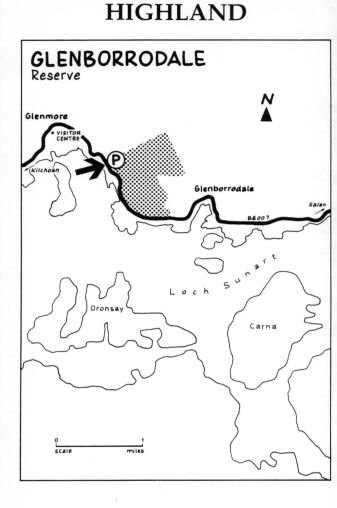

Location

Situated on the southern side of the Ardnamurchan peninsula, 1/2 mile (1 km) west of Glenborrodale village along the B8007. Access at NM/601608 and NM/593619.

Glenborrodale Nature Reserve is in a beautiful, but remote area. There is a circular nature trail with some difficult terrain.

Habitat
A varied reserve of 250 acres (101 ha) including loch shore, broadleaved woodland with herb rich glades, bogs and flushes, to heathland and upland blanket bog.

Birds
Wood warblers, tree pipits, redstarts, whitethroats, whinchats, stonechats and ravens all breed on the reserve. Merlins and golden eagles are seen occasionally.

Other wildlife
Otter, pine marten and Scottish wildcat are present, as are red and roe deer. There is also a colony of pearl-bordered fritillary butterflies.

Visiting
The nature trails are always open. Parking is possible at NM/593619. Please do not park in passing places.

Facilities
G

Warden
Present from April to August. Enquiries to RSPB North Scotland Office (page 295).

 Cameron Centre, Cameron Square, Fort William PH33 6AJ (tel: 0397 703781).

INSH MARSHES,
HIGHLAND

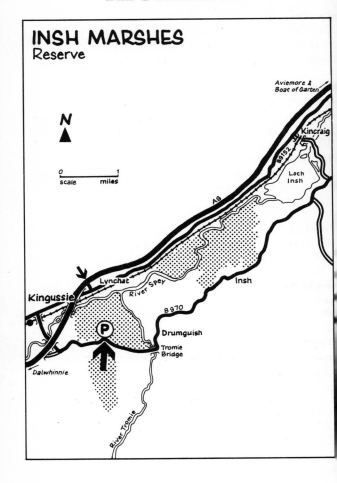

Location

Situated in Badenoch and Strathspey between Kingussie and Loch Insh, the reserve reception and car park is entered off the B970 road to Insh village 1¹/2 miles (2.4 km) from Kingussie. NH/775998. The nearest railway station is in Kingussie (1¹/2 miles - 2.4 km).

Stretching along the River Spey, two trails lead visitors through marshes, meadows and woodland. Ospreys are regularly seen fishing. There are two hides and a small information centre.

Habitat

Extensive marshes in the floodplain of the upper River Spey which usually flood in winter. Also sedge meadows with pools and willow scrub bordered by birch and juniper woodland from which extends some moorland into the foothills of the Cairngorms. The reserve covers 2,105 acres (851 ha).

Birds

Wigeons, teals, shovelers, tufted ducks, goldeneyes, curlews, redshanks and both sedge and grasshopper warblers all breed on the reserve. Woodcocks, great spotted woodpeckers, tree pipits and redstarts nest in the woodland with dippers and grey wagtails on the burns. Ospreys, hen harriers and buzzards are seen regularly. Large numbers of whooper swans visit the marshes in winter when greylag and pink-footed geese pass on migration.

Other wildlife

Otter and roe deer are present. Scotch argus is a notable butterfly.

Visiting

Open daily 9 am to 9 pm or sunset when earlier. Two hides overlook the marshes and two waymarked trails explore a variety of habitats.

Facilities

P   IC   G

Warden

Zul Bhatia, Ivy Cottage, Insh, Kingussie PH21 1NT.

i King Street, Kingussie, Highland (tel: 054 0661 297).

LOCH RUTHVEN,
HIGHLAND

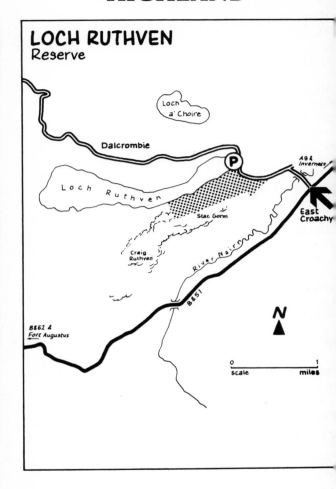

Location

Situated near Loch Ness to the south of Inverness, the reserve is reached from the A9 via the B851 road to East Croachy, turning north-west along a minor road for one mile (1.6 km). NH/637282. The nearest railway station is in Inverness (11 miles - 17.5 km).

This beautiful reserve is the best place to watch rare Slavonian grebes during the summer. There is a simple trail and hide overlooking the loch.

Habitat
Shallow loch shore with sedge beds as well as birchwoods, cliffs and crags and heather moorland covering 211 acres (85 ha).

Birds
The reserve is the most important nesting site in Britain for Slavonian grebes. Red-breasted mergansers, mallards, teal, tufted ducks, wigeons and coots also breed. The crags attract buzzards, kestrels and ravens. Black grouse, peregrines, hen harriers and ospreys are seen occasionally.

Other wildlife
Roe deer are present.

Visiting
Access at all times from the small car park (no parking on road please) to the hide which offers excellent views of the grebes in the breeding season. Otherwise please keep to the waymarked paths to avoid disturbing the grebes.

Facilities
P

Warden
Present from April to August. Enquiries to RSPB North Scotland Office (page 295).

i Castle Wynd, Inverness (tel: 0463 234353).

Slavonian grebe

UDALE BAY,

HIGHLAND

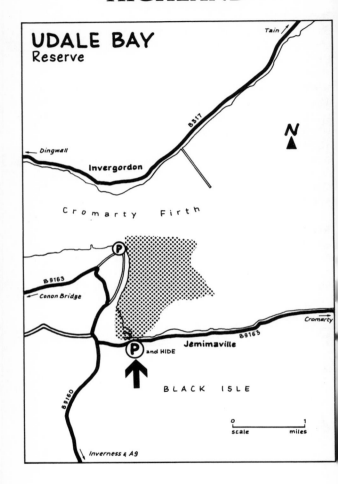

Location

On the north shore of the Black Isle, Udale Bay is entered from the car park to the west of Jemimaville on the B9163. NH/712651. The nearest railway station is in Dingwall (16 miles - 25 km).

A hide, accessible to wheelchairs, overlooks the mudflats of the Cromarty Firth. In the winter this is a good place to watch a range of wading birds and waterfowl.

Habitat
Mudflats with eel grass as well as saltmarsh, marshy grazing and scrub covering 778 acres (315 ha).

Birds
There are a large number of wigeons in the autumn and winter flocks of oystercatchers, knots, dunlins, bar-tailed godwits, curlews and redshanks. Greylag geese, pink-footed geese and whooper swans use the bay as a roost and a flock of scaups winter offshore from Jemimaville.

Visiting
Access at all times from the small car park to the hide which looks out over the mudflats.

Facilities

Warden
None present. Enquiries to RSPB North Scotland Office (page 295).

i Castle Wynd, Inverness (tel: 0463 234353).

BIRSAY MOORS AND COTTASGARTH,

ORKNEY

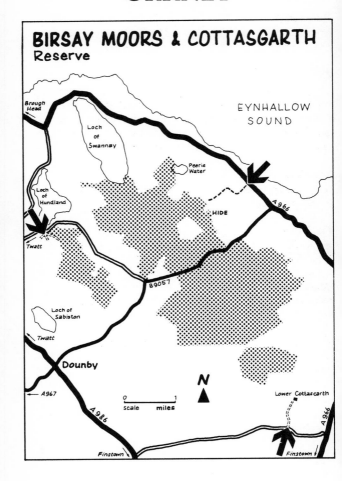

Location

Situated in the north of the Mainland of Orkney, this large reserve may be enjoyed from a number of points.

There are small hides at Cottasgarth and Burgar Hill, the latter with wheelchair access. As there are no formal paths on the moors, walking can be difficult, but good views can be obtained from the B9047. In the summer, hen harriers, great and arctic skuas and red-throated divers can be seen. A warden is occasionally at the reserve between April and September.

Habitat

The reserve covers 5,781 acres (2,339 ha) of undulating heather moorland on the Old Red Sandstone with blanket bog, marshy areas and streams.

Birds

There is an unusually high density of hen harriers that nest here with a few merlins and ground-nesting kestrels. There are also small colonies of both great and arctic skuas as well as great and lesser black-backed gulls. Other breeding species include oystercatchers, golden plovers, dunlins, stonechats and short-eared owls with several species of ducks.

Other wildlife

The Orkney vole is common. The Dee of Durkadale is rich in orchids and sedges.

Visiting

Access at all times. Cottasgarth has a small hide providing good views of the moorland birds, especially hen harriers. A hide by Burgar Hill, by the wind generators, is signposted from the A966 at Evie (HY/358266) and overlooks a red-throated diver breeding site. The Birsay Moors may be viewed from the B9057 road from Dounby to Evie. Dee of Durkadale is reached by turning right along the rough track at the south end of Loch Hundland to the ruined farm of Durkadale (HY/293252). Please close gates.

Facilities

G to Orkney reserves

Warden

Occasionally present from April to August. Enquiries to Keith Fairclough, Viewforth, Swannay, By Evie, Orkney KW17 2NR.

i Orkney Tourist Board, 6 Broad Street, Kirkwall (tel: 0856 872856).

Ferries and air

For ferry and air connections see page 231.

COPINSAY, ORKNEY

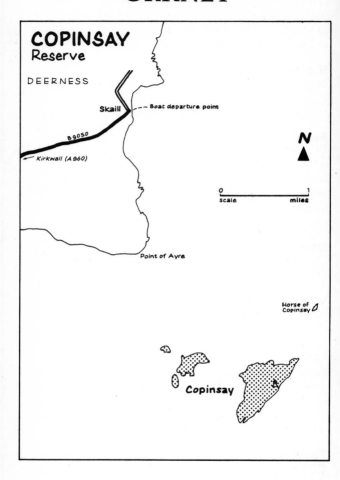

COPINSAY Reserve

DEERNESS

Skaill --- Boat departure point

B9050

← Kirkwall (A960)

Point of Ayre

Horse of Copinsay

Copinsay

N

0   1
scale   miles

Location
The James Fisher Memorial island two miles (3.2 km) off the east coast of Mainland Orkney near Skaill. HY/610010.

This beautiful island is two miles from the mainland of Orkney. The cliffs are home to large nesting colonies of seabirds, including fulmars, guillemots and kittiwakes. The island is reached by boat from Skaill.

Habitat
The reserve is a 375 acre (152 ha) island of Old Red Sandstone with almost a mile (1.6 km) of sheer cliffs, also rocky shores connecting it to islets.

Birds
Very large cliff-nesting colonies of kittiwakes, guillemots, razorbills and fulmars with some shags, puffins, black guillemots and cormorants. Both great and lesser black-backed gulls, arctic terns, rock doves, eiders, twites, ravens and occasionally corncrakes also breed. A good variety of passage migrants can be seen in spring and autumn during periods of easterly winds.

Other wildlife
There is a fine colony of oyster plant on the beach.

Visiting
Access at all times by taking day-trips to the island by boat from Skaill (contact S Foubister - tel: 085 674 252). Excellent views may be obtained of the cliff-nesting birds from several points but visitors are asked to take great care.

Facilities
G to Orkney reserves

Warden
None present. Enquiries to Keith Fairclough, Viewforth, Swannay, By Evie, Orkney KW17 2NR.

i Orkney Tourist Board, 6 Broad Street, Kirkwall (tel: 0856 872856).

Ferries
Run daily from Scrabster in Caithness to Stromness on Mainland Orkney. Enquiries to P&O Ferries, Orkney and Shetland Services, PO Box 5, Aberdeen AB9 8DL (tel: 0224 572615).

Air
There are flights from Edinburgh, etc. Enquiries to British Airways (tel: 0856 3356) or Loganair (tel: 0856 3457).

HOBBISTER,
ORKNEY

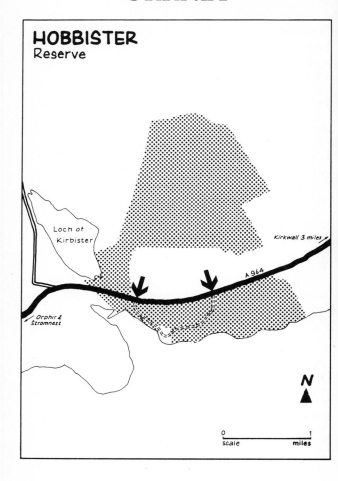

Location

Lying either side of the A964 road from Kirkwall to
Stromness near the village of Orphir on Orkney Mainland,
the reserve may be entered along a track at HY/396070 or
a minor road at HY/381068.

This reserve is a mixture of moorland, sandflats, saltmarsh and sea-cliffs. A few simple paths allow visitors to watch birds of prey and curlews. Walking elsewhere on the moorland is hard going.

Habitat

The habitat is predominantly heather moorland with bogs and fen and drained by the Swartaback Burn. There are also low sea-cliffs above the sandy Waulkmill Bay and a small area of saltmarsh. The reserve is 1,875 acres (759 ha) in size.

Birds

Hen harriers, short-eared owls, merlins, red grouse, curlews, snipe, red-throated divers and twites breed on the moorland with colonies of lesser black-backed and common gulls. Fulmars, ravens, eiders, red-breasted mergansers and black guillemots nest on the coast where divers and seaducks may be seen at other times.

Other wildlife

Round-leaved sundew, butterwort and bog asphodel flower in the bogs.

Visiting

Access at all times but please do not disturb the breeding divers and birds of prey. Waulkmill Bay provides some good birdwatching outside the breeding season.

Facilities

G to Orkney reserves

Warden

Only occasionally present. Enquiries to Keith Fairclough, Viewforth, Swannay, By Evie, Orkney KW17 2NR.

i Orkney Tourist Board, 6 Broad Street, Kirkwall (tel: 0856 872856).

Ferries and air

For ferry and air connections see page 231.

THE LOONS,
ORKNEY

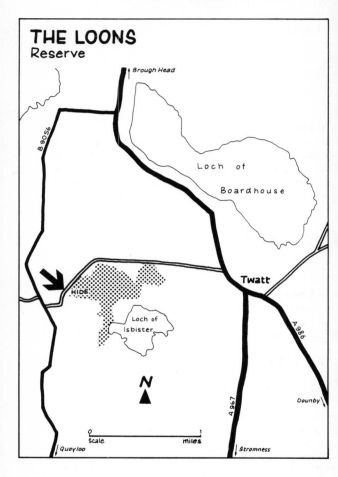

Location

Situated in the north of Mainland Orkney beside the Loch of Isbister, the reserve is approached along the minor road from the A986 three miles (4.8 km) north of Dounby.

A hide overlooks this marshland reserve, where red-breasted mergansers and redshanks breed in the summer and geese spend the winter. To avoid unnecessary disturbance to nesting birds, there is no access to the reserve (apart from the hide) during the breeding season.

Habitat
A marsh of 139 acres (56 ha) within a basin of Old Red Sandstone hills, containing old peat workings and bordered by a loch.

Birds
Teals, shovelers, wigeons, pintails, red-breasted mergansers, snipe and redshanks breed here as well as colonies of common and black-headed gulls and arctic terns. Corncrakes occur occasionally. A regular flock of Greenland white-fronted geese and several species of ducks visit in winter.

Other wildlife
Grass of Parnassus, alpine meadow-rue and several species of orchids flower here. Otters are also seen.

Visiting
Access at all times to the hide on the west side of the reserve (HY/246242).

Facilities
G to Orkney reserves

Warden
None regularly present. Enquiries to Keith Fairclough, Viewforth, Swannay, By Evie, Orkney KW17 2NR.

i Orkney Tourist Board, 6 Broad Street, Kirkwall (tel: 0856 872856).

Ferries and air
For ferry and air connections see page 231.

Eider

Scotland's Treasure Islands

Experience Orkney. A scattering of Scottish Islands with a treasure trove of history and archaeology.

A wealth of wildlife that's a paradise for the bird watcher.

And a warm and genuine welcome in our hotels, inns, guest houses and self catering cottages.

Orkney. A holiday you'll always treasure.

Phone 0856 872856 now for your free brochure or send the coupon now.

MAJOR NATURE RESERVES

1	North Hoy
2	Marwick Head
3	The Loons
4	Hobbister
5	Trumland
6	Copinsay

- -

To: Brenda Rice, Orkney Tourist Board,
6 Broad Street, Kirkwall, Orkney KW15 1NX.

Name ....

Address ....

....

....

MARWICK HEAD,
ORKNEY

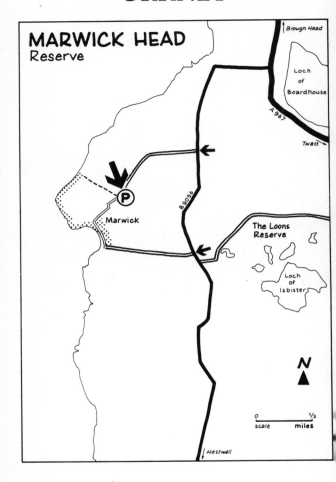

Location
On the west coast of Mainland Orkney north of
Marwick Bay to which a minor road runs from the B9056.
HY/232249.

Close to The Loons Reserve, the spectacular 300-foot (90-metre) cliffs provide breeding sites for thousands of seabirds. The sight, sound and smell of this seabird city is breathtaking. There is a path to the cliff-top from the car park.

Habitat
One mile (1.6 km) of sheer cliffs of Old Red Sandstone, rising almost to 300 ft (90 m), on which there are numerous ledges for nesting seabirds. Part of the rocky bay of Marwick and some wet meadowland are also within the reserve.

Birds
The reserve has the most spectacular seabird breeding colony on Mainland Orkney, holding very large populations of guillemots and kittiwakes. Razorbills, fulmars, rock doves, ravens and wheatears also nest here.

Other wildlife
Thrift, sea campion and spring squill provide a fine show of flowers. Both grey and common seals may be seen.

Visiting
Access at all times by walking from the car park at Cumlaquoy (HY/232252), alternatively from the road end at Marwick Bay (HY/229242). The seabirds may be viewed well from the cliff-top, but visitors are cautioned to take great care.

Facilities
G to Orkney reserves

Warden
None present. Enquiries to Keith Fairclough, Viewforth, Swannay, By Evie, Orkney KW17 2NR.

i Orkney Tourist Board, 6 Broad Street, Kirkwall (tel: 0856 872856).

Ferries and air
For details of ferries and air connections see page 231.

MILL DAM, SHAPINSAY, ORKNEY

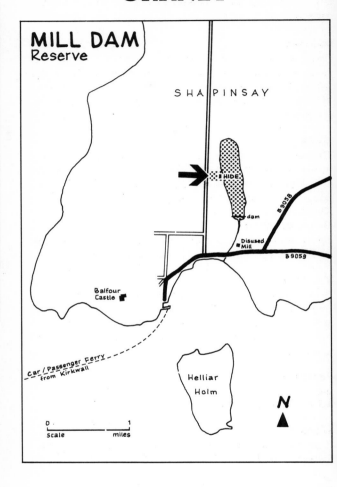

Location

Situated in the south-west quarter of the island of Shapinsay, it is best viewed from the minor road to the west which looks down onto the marsh. HY/481177.

A hide, with wheelchair access, overlooks the swamp where breeding pintails, teals and other ducks can be seen. Shapinsay can be reached from Kirkwall by a 25-minute ferry journey and the reserve is a short walk from the pier.

Habitat
Thirty-nine acres (16 ha) of swamp fen with some open water. Water levels controlled by a sluice at the dam.

Birds
The reserve has breeding pintails, shovelers, wigeons, tufted ducks, teals, coots, moorhens and mallards. As well as curlews, snipe, redshanks and oystercatchers, about 400 pairs of black-headed gulls also breed. Up to 120 whooper swans and good numbers of other wildfowl winter here.

Other wildlife
Otters are occasionally seen.

Visiting
Access at all times. The reserve lies just a short walk from the pier.

Facilities
G to Orkney reserves

Warden
Honorary warden: Paul Hollinrake, Farrowend, Shapinsay, Orkney.

i Orkney Tourist Board, 6 Broad Street, Kirkwall (tel: 0856 872856).

Ferries
A car/passenger ferry sails from Kirkwall several times per day in the summer months.

NORTH HILL, PAPA WESTRAY,
ORKNEY

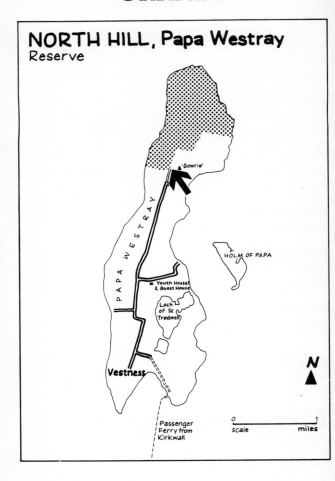

NORTH HILL, Papa Westray
Reserve

'Gowrie'

PAPA WESTRAY

HOLM OF PAPA

Youth Hostel & Guest House

Loch of St Tredwell

Vestness

Passenger Ferry from Kirkwall

N

0   scale   1
miles

Location
The reserve occupies the northern part of this small Orkney
island with its entrance at the north end of the principal
road. HY/496538.

Reached by ferry or plane from Kirkwall, the reserve is 3 miles (5 km) from the pier at the north end of the island. There is a simple perimeter path around the reserve where arctic terns and arctic skuas among other birds breed. A warden is present from April to August and conducts regular escorted walks.

Habitat
There is a large maritime heath of sedge, heather, crowberry and creeping willow bordered by a rocky coastline with some low sandstone cliffs covering 510 acres (206 ha).

Birds
An exceptionally large colony of arctic terns nests on the heath close to arctic skuas, eiders, ringed plovers, oystercatchers, dunlins, wheatears and four species of gulls. Black guillemots, razorbills, guillemots, puffins, kittiwakes, shags and rock doves inhabit the cliffs. Several migrant species occur including some rarities.

Other wildlife
Scottish primrose, alpine meadow-rue, mountain everlasting and frog orchid are notable plants.

Visiting
Access at all times but visitors are asked to contact the summer warden on arrival, preferably having arranged in advance an escorted tour to view the nesting colonies. These may be viewed well from the perimeter path.

Facilities
G to Orkney reserves

Warden
Present from mid-April to mid-August, c/o Rose Cottage, Papa Westray KW17 2BU (tel: 085 74 240).

i Orkney Tourist Board, 6 Broad Street, Kirkwall (tel: 0856 872856).

NORTH HOY,
ORKNEY

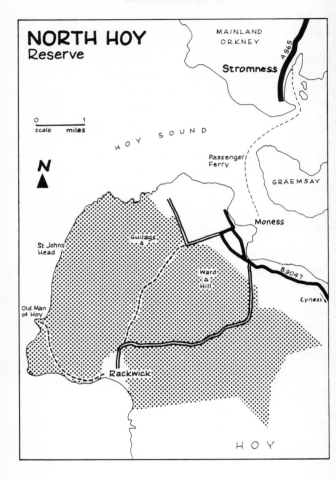

Location

Occupying the north-west part of the island of Hoy around Ward Hill, the reserve is reached either by passenger ferry from Stromness to Moness pier then a short walk to the reserve boundary (HY/223034), or by car ferry from Houton to Lyness then up the B9047 road to Rackwick ND/203995.

North Hoy is a mixture of moorland and cliffs, including the famous Old Man of Hoy rock stack. The island of Hoy is reached by a short passenger ferry crossing from Stromness or car ferry from Houton to Lyness. A number of paths cross the reserve and there is an information display in the Hoy Inn.

Habitat
A large plateau 9,700 acres (3,925 ha) of moorland, dissected by glacial valleys, and varying from heather and deer grass to mountain heath and sub-Arctic vegetation on the summit. The reserve also contains several miles of spectacular cliffs rising to 1,100 ft (335 m) at St John's Head.

Birds
A large population of great skuas breeds on the moorland with red grouse, golden plovers, dunlins, curlews, hen harriers, merlins, short-eared owls, twites, great black-backed gulls and arctic skuas. Guillemots, razorbills, kittiwakes, shags, peregrines and ravens nest on the cliffs with a colony of Manx shearwaters nearby.

Other wildlife
Alpine plants such as purple saxifrage, moss campion and Alpine saw-wort grow in the gullies and on ledges. Mountain hares are present.

Visiting
Access at all times, there being a footpath through the glen between Ward Hill and Cuilags and another from the village of Rackwick to the famous Old Man of Hoy rock stack. Visitors are warned to take special care on the cliff-tops which are crumbly. There is an information display at the Hoy Inn near Moness.

Facilities
IC   **G** to Orkney reserves

Warden
Tom Prescott, Ley House, North Hoy, Orkney KW16 3NJ.

i Orkney Tourist Board, 6 Broad Street, Kirkwall (tel: 0856 872856).

Taxis or hire-cars
Are available on the island - enquire at the pier.

NOUP CLIFFS,

ORKNEY

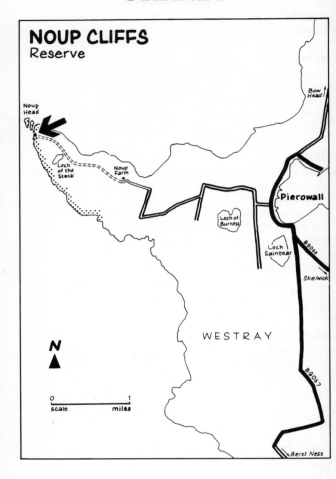

Location

Forming the western promontory of the island of Westray, the cliffs are approached from Pierowall along the minor road to Noup Farm then the track to the lighthouse at the north end of the reserve. HY/392500.

The cliffs of the reserve form one of the largest seabird colonies in Britain. The reserve is not that easy to reach by foot, but visitors can park at Noup Head lighthouse and walk 2.5 km along the cliff where good views of the birds can be obtained. The island is reached by ferry from Kirkwall.

Habitat
One and a half miles (2.4 km) of high sandstone sea-cliffs with numerous ledges and backed by maritime heath (off the reserve).

Birds
This is one of the largest seabird colonies in the British Isles with immense numbers of guillemots and kittiwakes. Razorbills, puffins, shags, fulmars, rock pipits and ravens also breed.

Other wildlife
Grey seals and occasionally porpoises and dolphins are seen offshore.

Visiting
Access at all times to the cliff-top (please take great care) from where excellent views may be obtained of the seabirds. Visitors are asked to close gates on the access track.

Facilities
G to Orkney reserves

Warden
None present. Enquiries to Keith Fairclough, Viewforth, Swannay, By Evie, Orkney KW17 2NR.

i Orkney Tourist Board, 6 Broad Street, Kirkwall (tel: 0856 872856).

Ferries or air
The island is reached by passenger ferry from Kirkwall or by air service from Kirkwall airport. Enquiries to Loganair (tel: 0856 2494).

TRUMLAND, ROUSAY, ORKNEY

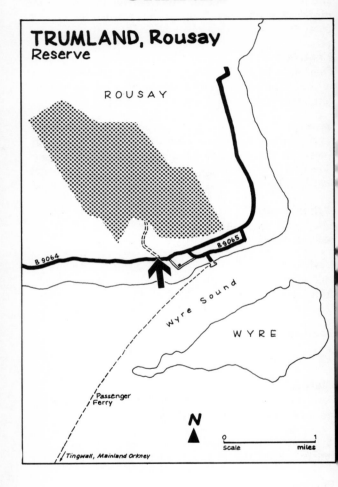

TRUMLAND, Rousay
Reserve

ROUSAY

B 9064

B 9065

Wyre Sound

WYRE

Passenger
Ferry

N

0 scale 1 miles

Tingwall, Mainland Orkney

Location

The reserve lies above Trumland House in the south of the island of Rousay which is reached by passenger ferry from Tingwall off the A966 road in the north-east of Mainland Orkney. HY/427276.

This moorland reserve is reached by ferry from Tingwall on Mainland Orkney. The start of the nature trail is just 1/2 mile (1 km) from the pier. A trail guide gives information about the walks. A warden is present from April to August.

Habitat

Mainly heather moorland rising to 800 ft (244 m) at Blotchnie Field, dissected by small valleys and containing a lochan and some crags known as 'hamars'. The reserve is 1,070 acres (433 ha) in size.

Birds

Red-throated divers, hen harriers, kestrels and golden plovers breed and short-eared owls, merlins and both great and arctic skuas may be seen. A mixed colony of herring and lesser black-backed gulls is located on the moorland where both great black-backed and common gulls also nest.

Other wildlife

Orkney voles are present and otters visit the reserve occasionally.

Visiting

Access at all times, but visitors are asked to contact the summer warden who will escort them. A shop and public toilets are located in the village near the pier.

Facilities

WC   **G** to Orkney reserves

Warden

Present from April to August at Trumland Mill Cottage, Rousay, Orkney. Otherwise enquiries to Keith Fairclough, Viewforth, Swannay, By Evie, Orkney KW17 2NR.

i Orkney Tourist Board, 6 Broad Street, Kirkwall (tel: 0856 872856).

Ferries or air

For details of ferries and flights see page 231.

FETLAR,
SHETLAND

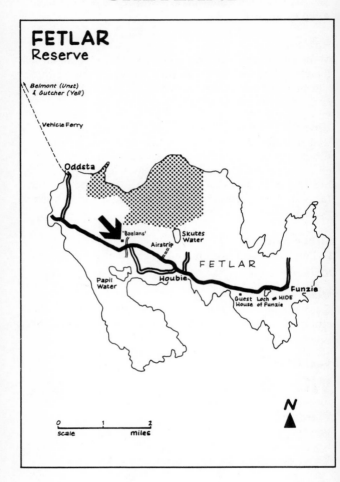

Location

Being the smallest of the three inhabited northern islands of Shetland, Fetlar is reached by public ferry from Yell and Unst. Another ferry connects Yell to the Mainland of Shetland.

Fetlar was once famous for its breeding snowy owls, and one or two non-breeding birds are usually present. The island has almost all of Britain's breeding red-necked phalaropes and large numbers of whimbrels, skuas and terns.

Habitat

Most of the reserve consists of grassy heathland encompassing the summits of Vord Hill and Stackaberg, and bordered by high sea-cliffs and boulder shores to the north and crofting areas in the south. The heather moor and blanket bog of the west of Fetlar contrasts with some dry heath in the east. The reserve covers 1,700 acres (688 ha).

Birds

Fetlar's breeding birds include Manx shearwaters, storm petrels, shags, eiders, red-throated divers, golden plovers, dunlins, snipes, curlews, ravens, twites and whimbrels. Red-necked phalaropes feeding on the Loch of Funzie (HU/658897) may be watched from the road or a hide. Many passage migrants including rarities occur in spring and autumn.

Other wildlife

Common and grey seals and otters frequent the coast.

Visiting

Visitors are welcome to the island all year, but the reserve and sanctuary may not be entered in summer other than by arrangement with the warden, who escorts parties to view the snowy owls. Baelans is signposted 2 1/2 miles from the Oddsta ferry terminal (HU/604916). Visitors are asked not to disturb the breeding birds and to respect the property of farmers and crofters.

Facilities

G to Shetland reserves

Warden

Present from April to September at Baelans, Fetlar ZE2 9DJ. Otherwise enquiries to RSPB Shetland Office (page 295).

i Shetland Islands Tourism, Market Cross, Lerwick, Shetland (tel: 0595 693434).

See page 253 for details of ferries and flights to Shetland.

A bus from Lerwick connects with the public ferry but does not cross to Fetlar. Advance booking of vehicles for the ferry is essential (tel: 095 782 259/268).

LOCH OF SPIGGIE,
SHETLAND

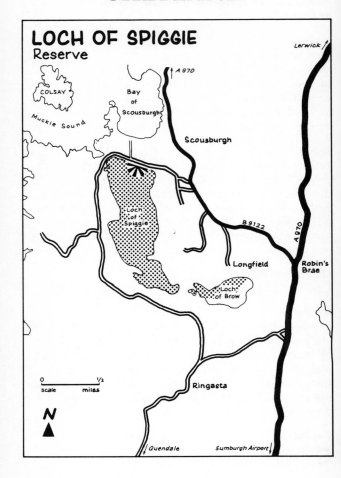

Location

Situated near the southern end of Mainland Shetland, the reserve is approached by turning off the B9122 road near Scousburgh which is west of the A970 from Lerwick four miles (6.4 km) north of Sumburgh airport.

In the autumn and winter, flocks of whooper swans stop off on their migration south. In spring and summer, look for roosting long-tailed ducks and bathing terns and great skuas. Good views of the reserve can be obtained from the surrounding roads.

Habitat
This 284-acre (115-ha) reserve comprises a shallow freshwater loch separated from the sea by sand dunes and from the neighbouring Loch of Brow (partly in the reserve) by a marsh.

Birds
Teals, shelducks, oystercatchers and curlews nest in the area while the loch is often used for bathing by arctic terns, both great and arctic skuas and kittiwakes. Long-tailed ducks gather to display on the loch in spring. As many as 300 whooper swans winter here regularly as well as greylag geese, tufted ducks, pochards, goldeneyes and wigeons.

Other wildlife
Otters are resident.

Visiting
The reserve may not be entered, but good views of the loch are obtained from the minor road at the north end HU/373176. Please do not impede other road-users.

Warden
None regularly present. Enquiries to the RSPB Shetland Office (page 295).

i Shetland Islands Tourism, Market Cross, Lerwick, Shetland (tel: 0595 693434).

Ferries or air
Shetland may be reached by car ferry from Aberdeen or Orkney or by air from Edinburgh, Aberdeen, Inverness and Orkney. Enquiries to British Airways (tel: 031 225 2525). Ferry enquiries to P&O Ferries, Orkney and Shetland Services, PO Box 5, Aberdeen AB9 8DL (tel: 0224 572615). A bus from Lerwick to Sumburgh can disembark passengers at Robin's Brae, two miles (3.2 km) from the reserve.

LUMBISTER,
SHETLAND

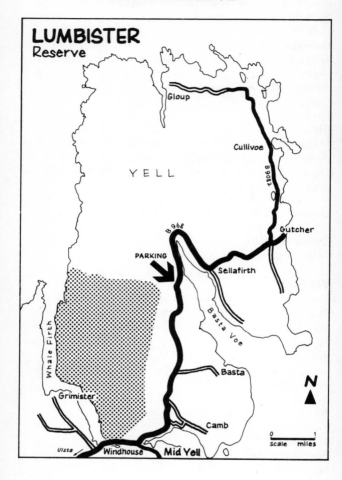

LUMBISTER
Reserve

Gloup

Cullivoe

B9082

YELL

B968

Gutcher

PARKING

Sellafirth

Basta Voe

Whale Firth

Basta

N

Grimister

Camb

scale   miles

Ulsta   Windhouse   Mid Yell

Location

Occupies the west side of the island of Yell between Whale
Firth and the A968 road to Gutcher.

Situated on the island of Yell, this reserve is a mixture of moorland and shore. A rough footpath to the Dall of Lumbister offers the best access to see breeding waders and skuas.

Habitat

Extensive, undulating moorland of heather and bog broken by many water-bodies as well as a steep gorge leading to the rugged grass-topped cliffs and rocky shore of Whale Firth. It covers 4,000 acres (1,617 ha).

Birds

Red-throated divers, red-breasted mergansers and eiders nest on the loch while merlins and both arctic and great skuas breed on the moorland with golden plovers, curlews, dunlins and twites. Ravens, wheatears, rock doves, puffins and black guillemots nest on the cliffs.

Other wildlife

Otters are common and both grey and common seals may be seen offshore. Lesser twayblade grows in the bogs and juniper and roseroot in the gorge.

Visiting

Good views may be obtained from the A968 road. Pedestrian access is gained from the lay-by four miles (6.4 km) north of Mid Yell (HU/509974) but visitors are asked to take care not to disturb the divers and other breeding birds.

Facilities

G to Shetland reserves

Warden

Occasionally present during summer. Enquiries to RSPB Shetland Office (page 295).

i Shetland Islands Tourism, Market Cross, Lerwick, Shetland (tel: 0595 693434).

Ferry

A car ferry operates between Mainland Shetland and the island of Yell. See also page 253.

Wales

Wheatear

CWM CLYDACH,

WEST GLAMORGAN

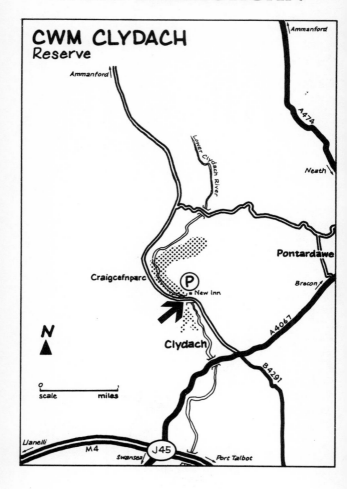

Location

Take the minor road up the river valley from Clydach which lies off the A4067 road from Swansea north-east of its junction with the M4. The reserve car park lies two miles (3.2 km) north of Clydach at the New Inn public house. SN/685026. The nearest railway station is Swansea (10 miles - 16 km).

Waymarked paths lead visitors along the river through this south Wales wooded valley.

Habitat
Oak woodland lines the banks of the lower River Clydach with smaller areas of birch and beech and wetter ground containing ash and alder. Heather and bracken slopes lie above the woodland. The reserve covers 176 acres (72 ha).

Birds
Nesting buzzards, sparrowhawks and ravens are frequently seen. Nestboxes are used by pied flycatchers, redstarts and tits while wood warblers, all three species of woodpecker, nuthatches, treecreepers and tawny owls also nest in the woods. Dippers and grey wagtails frequent the river and tree pipits and wheatears the higher ground. Snipe, woodcocks, redpolls and siskins are plentiful in winter.

Other wildlife
Badger and fox are present. The many species of butterflies include purple hairstreak and silver-washed fritillary.

Visiting
Access at all times to a waymarked path along the riverside, beginning at the New Inn public house. Visitors are asked to keep strictly to this footpath.

Facilities
P

Warden
Martin Humphreys, 2 Tyn y Berllan, Craig Cefn Parc, Clydach, Swansea, West Glamorgan SA6 5TL.

i PO Box 59, Singleton Street, Swansea, West Glamorgan SA1 3QG.

Badger

DINAS and GWENFFRWD, DYFED

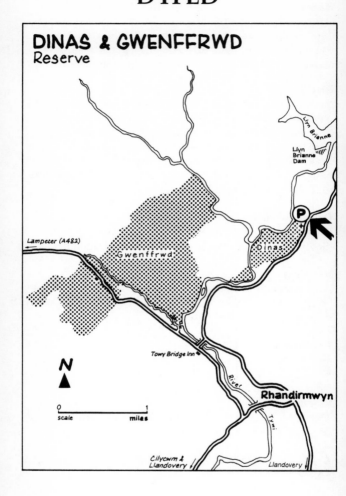

Location

Lying in the Tywi valley of the central Welsh hills, Dinas reserve is entered off the road to the Llyn Brianne dam north of Rhandirmwyn village. SN/788472. For access to the Gwenffrwd part of the reserve see below. The nearest railway station is Llandovery (10 miles - 16 km).

These two woodland reserves offer pleasant walks through typical Welsh oakwoods. The visitor centre at Dinas is open during the summer. The Dinas path is rugged in places.

Habitat

This 1,723-acre (697 ha) reserve comprises hillside oakwoods with rocky outcrops, streams and bracken slopes rising to heather and grass moorland with valley fields and riverside woodland.

Birds

Buzzards, sparrowhawks, kestrels, ravens and red kites are seen in the area particularly in spring. Many woodland nestboxes are used by pied flycatchers. Redstarts, wood warblers, nuthatches, woodcocks, tits and woodpeckers also breed. Grey wagtails, common sandpipers and dippers frequent the rivers, tree pipits and whinchats the hillsides and wheatears and red grouse the moorland.

Other wildlife

Polecats are seen occasionally. Salmon and trout inhabit the river.

Visiting

The Dinas nature trail is accessible at all times from the car park where an information centre is open in summer. The terrain is rough and steep in places. For enjoyment of the four mile (6.4 km) hill nature trail at Gwenffrwd, visitors should to go to the Dinas visitor centre first (10 am to 5 pm), Easter - August.

Facilities

P IC G s

Warden

Tony Pickup, Troedrhiwgelynen, Rhandirmwyn, Llandovery SA20 0PN.

i Central Car Park, Broad Street, Llandovery, Dyfed SA20 0AR.

DYFFRYN WOOD,
POWYS

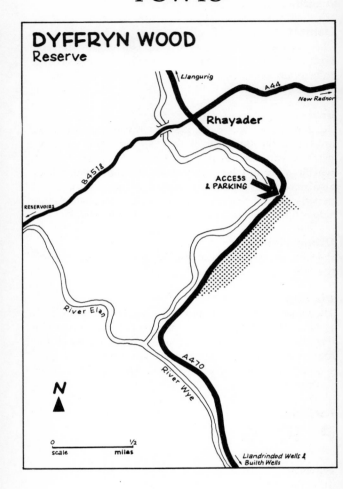

DYFFRYN WOOD
Reserve

Llangurig

A44

New Radnor

Rhayader

B4518

ACCESS & PARKING

RESERVOIRS

River Elan

A470

River Wye

N

0   ½
scale   miles

Llandrindod Wells &
Builth Wells

Location

Forming part of the composite RSPB reserve holding in
the upper reaches of the rivers Wye and Elan, this wood
lies beside the A470 road to Builth Wells just south of
Rhayader. SN/980672. The nearest railway station is
Llandrindod Wells (11 miles - 18 km).

A circular path leads visitors round this fine example of ungrazed oakwood.

Habitat
A hillside oak woodland with an area of heather, gorse and bracken and rocky ravines covering 77 acres (31 ha).

Birds
Pied flycatchers, wood warblers and redstarts breed plentifully with a few pairs of ravens and buzzards, while grey wagtails and dippers nest along the rocky streams. Whinchats and stonechats frequent the upper woodland fringe where there is the possibility of seeing birds of prey such as peregrines and red kites.

Other wildlife
Badger, polecat, fox and common lizard may be seen. The woodland and ravines are rich in mosses, liverworts and lichens.

Visiting
Access at all times to the woodland walk starting at the lay-by at the north end of the wood.

Warden
c/o Dinas and Gwenffrwd nature reserve page 261.

i Leisure Centre, North Street, Rhayader, Powys (tel: 0597 810591).

Pied flycatcher

GRASSHOLM,
DYFED

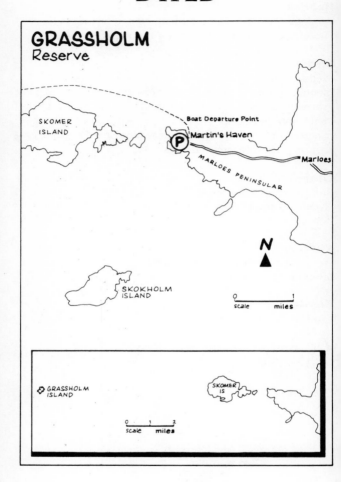

Location
Lies ten miles off the coast of west Wales and beyond the other bird-rich Pembrokeshire islands of Skomer and Skokholm. SM/599093. The nearest railway station is Milford Haven (12 miles - 19 km).

Grassholm is famous for its large colony of nesting gannets. To allow them to breed without disturbance visitors can only land on the island after 15 June. Visitors are advised that landing conditions are difficult, although excellent views of the birds can be had from the sea. There are no facilities on the reserve.

Habitat
An isolated, rocky island (22 acres - 9 ha) rising to 150 ft (45 m) above sea level.

Birds
Grassholm is renowned for its immense breeding colony of gannets numbering over 30,000 pairs, making it the second largest gannetry in the British Isles. There are also small numbers of guillemots, razorbills, shags, kittiwakes, herring gulls, great black-backed gulls and oystercatchers. Manx shearwaters may be seen over the sea.

Visiting
The island is inaccessible except in very calm weather. Boat landings are permitted only from 15 June onwards so that the gannets are not disturbed while incubating their eggs. There is a boat service from Martin's Haven (SM/761090) on the Marloes peninsula: further details from RSPB Wales Office (page 295). The gannets can be viewed well on the island from outside the sanctuary area which is demarcated by posts.

Honorary warden
David Saunders, c/o Dyfed Wildlife Trust, 7 Market Street, Haverfordwest, Dyfed (tel: 0437 5462).

i Old Bridge, Haverfordwest, Dyfed SA61 2EZ (tel: 0437 763110).

LAKE VYRNWY,
POWYS

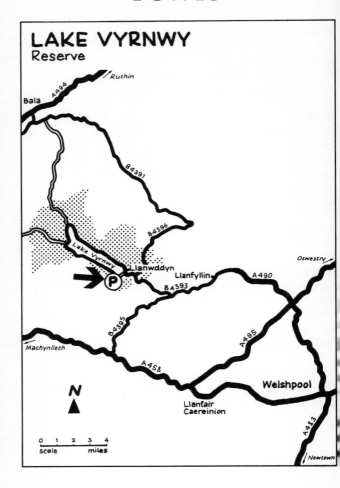

Location

This reservoir lies in the Berwyn hills west of Llanfyllin from where the visitor centre by the dam is reached via the B4393 road to Llanwddyn. SJ/020193. The nearest railway station is in Welshpool (21 miles - 34 km).

This reserve is popular with birdwatchers and families alike as it offers a full range of facilities. There are a number of nature trails, hides and a visitor centre with shop and toilets.

Habitat

Extensive heather moorland with conifer plantations, mixed deciduous woodland and sessile oakwoods, meadows and rocky streams surrounding Lake Vyrnwy reservoir. The reserve covers 17,720 acres (7,170 ha).

Birds

Goosanders, grey wagtails, common sandpipers, dippers and kingfishers nest by the lake and rocky streams. The mixed deciduous woodland contains nuthatches, treecreepers, sparrowhawks, chiffchaffs, garden warblers and both green and great spotted woodpeckers, while the sessile oakwoods are favoured by redstarts, wood warblers and pied flycatchers. Crossbills and siskins nest in the conifers. Ravens, buzzards, merlins and hen harriers frequent the moorland where wheatears, ring ouzels and curlews breed.

Other wildlife

Red squirrels and polecats are present. The many species of butterflies include pearl-bordered and silver-washed fritillaries.

Visiting

Visitors may travel around the reservoir by car. There are paths which may be walked, as well as a hide by the north-west shore. Three woodland nature trails, including a hide, are accessible at all times, and there is another hide by the car park which is suitable for wheelchairs. The visitor centre and RSPB shop in the old chapel are open daily (10.30 am - 5.30 pm) April - 24 December; and weekends only January - March.

Facilities

P WC IC ♿ **G S**

Warden

Mike Walker, Bryn Awel, Llanwddyn, Oswestry, Salop FY10 7LF.

i The Old School, Church Street, Oswestry, Salop (tel: 0691 662753).

MAWDDACH VALLEY,
GWYNEDD

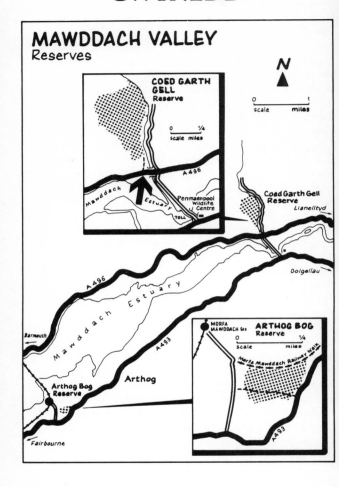

Location

Situated in the south of Snowdonia, this composite reserve comprises several properties around the Mawddach Estuary. Coed Garth Gell is reached up the public footpath from the A496 Barmouth to Dolgellau Road, starting opposite the Borthwnog Hall Hotel. Arthog Bog may be viewed from the scenic Morfa Mawddach railway walk near the mouth of the estuary. The nearest railway stations are Barmouth (7 miles - 11 km) and Mawddach (adjacent).

There are two parts to this reserve, which is set in beautiful estuary scenery, with a visitor centre at Penmaenpool. The trail at Arthog is accessible to wheelchair users.

Habitat

Coed Garth Gell is a hillside sessile oak and birch wood with open areas above a river gorge. Arthog Bog contains willow and alder scrub with pasture beside a raised mire. Coed Garth Gell is 166 acres (67 ha) and Arthog Bog 12 acres (4.8 ha).

Birds

Buzzards, ravens, pied flycatchers, wood warblers, lesser spotted woodpeckers, grey wagtails and dippers all breed at Coed Garth Cell. A few black grouse occur here in winter. Whitethroats, sedge and grasshopper warblers and occasionally lesser spotted woodpeckers nest at Arthog Bog which water rails visit in winter.

Other wildlife

Coed Garth is rich in bryophytes and lichens and numbers small pearl-bordered and dark green fritillaries among its butterflies. Greater spearwort and marsh cinquefoil occur at Arthog Bog.

Visiting

Access at all times. For Coed Garth Gell cars should be parked in the lay-by on the A496 (SH/687191) and for Arthog Bog in the Morfa Mawddach station car park (AS/630138). The Penmaenpool Wildlife Centre (see map) is open daily during Easter week and Whitsun - early September (11 am - 5 pm), but weekdays only Easter - Whitsun (12 pm - 4 pm).

Facilities

P IC &

Warden

Reg Thorpe, Abergwynant Lodge, Dolgellau, Gwynedd LL40 1YF (tel: 0341 422888).

i Ty Meirion, Eldon Square, Dolgellau LL40 1PU.

POINT OF AIR,
CLWYD

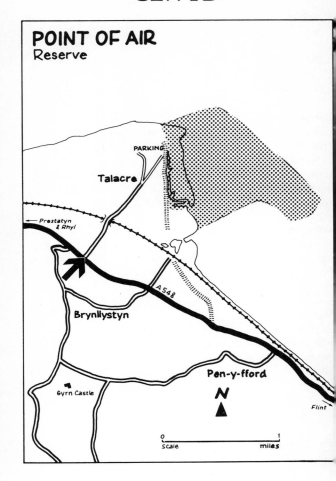

Location

Lying at the mouth of the Dee Estuary on the Welsh side,
a vantage point for this reserve is located at the end of
Station Road, Talacre, which is reached off the coastal
A548 road two miles (3.2 km) east of Prestatyn. SJ/113833.
The nearest railway station is Prestatyn (2 miles - 3.2 km).

This reserve overlooks the mudflats of the Dee Estuary. A single hide can be visited.

Habitat
Tidal mudflats with a shingle spit and a small area of saltmarsh covering 600 acres (243 ha).

Birds
Up to 20,000 waders roost here in winter, particularly oystercatchers, curlews, knots, dunlins and redshanks, while ringed plovers and sanderlings occur on migration. Mallards, shelducks, teals, wigeons, pintails and red-breasted mergansers also winter, when snow buntings, twites and occasionally Lapland buntings and shore larks frequent the shingle spit. Several species of terns occur in summer.

Visiting
Access at all times, with limited car parking space on the landward side only of the sea-wall. A public hide, situated at the edge of British Coal land and overlooking the Point, is accessible at all times only via the sea-wall running south. Visitors are asked not to disturb roosting waders and should not go onto the mudflats when the tide is rising.

Warden
Andrew Gouldstone, c/o RSPB Wales Office (page 295).

i Scala Cinema, High Street, Prestatyn, Clywd LL19 9LH (tel: 0745 854365).

Redshank

RAMSEY ISLAND, DYFED

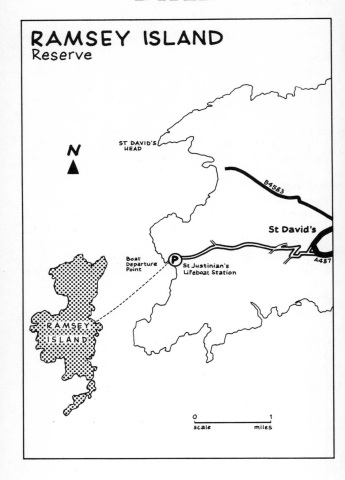

Location

The island is situated one mile (1.6 km) off the coast of Pembrokeshire, near St David's. It is reached by boat from St Justinians' Lifeboat Station. SM/702240. The nearest railway station is in Fishguard (20 miles - 32 km).

Ramsey Island is a breeding stronghold for choughs, a rare member of the crow family. Information and some refreshments are available on the island. Daily boats run during the summer allowing about five hours on the island.

Habitat
Maritime heath dominates the southern part of Ramsey while a number of fields enclosed by traditional Pembrokeshire banks characterise the north of the island which is 625 acres (253 ha) in size.

Birds
The island is particularly notable for breeding choughs. Guillemots, razorbills and kittiwakes also nest on the cliffs. Wheatears nest in the traditional Pembrokeshire banks and lapwings occupy the small grass fields.

Other wildlife
The beaches and caves of Ramsey are the Welsh stronghold for Atlantic seals. Between late August and mid-November over 400 pups are born. Typical cliff-top plants such as thrift, spring squill and sea campion provide a colourful display in early summer.

Visiting
By boat from the Lifeboat Station at St Justinians near St David's. Every day, April to October, weather permitting. 10 am and 11 am returning at 3.30 pm (no visiting on Tuesdays). Visitor numbers are limited to 40 per day to keep disturbance of the wildlife to a minimum.

Facilities
WC IC G

Warden
Ian Bullock/Sue Ward, Tegfan, Caerbwdi, St Davids, Pembrokeshire SA62 6QP.

i Old Bridge, Haverfordwest, Dyfed SA61 3EZ (tel: 0437 763110).

Charitable trusts

- Help us save the countryside for the future

• For over a century, the RSPB has fought to conserve our natural heritage and protect the environment.

• As the largest wildlife conservation charity in Europe, we buy and manage nature reserves for wildlife, and fight to protect endangered species.

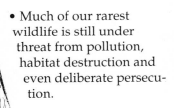

• Much of our rarest wildlife is still under threat from pollution, habitat destruction and even deliberate persecution.

• The RSPB will fight for a better future for our birds and the countryside - will you help?

If you administer a charitable trust and are interested in funding conservation, call us on 0767 680551.

RSPB

SOUTH STACK CLIFFS, GWYNEDD

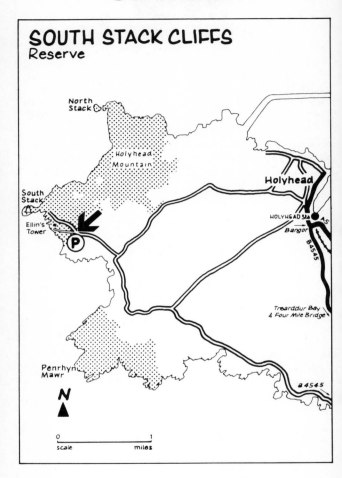

Location

Forming the western headland of Anglesey, the cliffs are signposted by road from both Holyhead and Trearddur Bay. SH/210818. The nearest railway is in Holyhead (3 1/2 miles - 5.6 km).

South Stack Cliffs is an ideal reserve to watch seabirds. Live video pictures of breeding seabirds are shown in the cliff-top information centre during the summer.

Habitat
High cliffs with caves and offshore stacks, backed by the maritime heathland of Holyhead Mountain covering 780 acres (316 ha).

Birds
Several pairs of choughs occupy these cliffs whose ledges are used by thousands of guillemots, razorbills and kittiwakes as well as several puffins. Ravens, jackdaws, shags and one or two pairs of peregrines also nest here, with stonechats and whitethroats on the heath. Manx shearwaters and gannets pass offshore and sometimes unusual species like pomarine skua.

Other wildlife
Silver-studded blue butterflies occur. The cliff-tops are colourful in the spring with thrift and spring squill, and spotted rock rose is a speciality.

Visiting
Access at all times to the car park from where a short track leads to Ellin's Tower, the information centre with a panoramic view of the cliffs and seabirds. A closed-circuit television system relays live pictures of the seabirds from April to August. Other car parks are also available.

Facilities
P WC IC G

Warden
Alastair Moralee, Swn-y-Môr, South Stack, Holyhead, Gwynedd LL65 3HB.

i Marine Square, Salt Island Approach, Holyhead, Gwynedd LL65 1DR (tel: 0407 762622).

VALLEY LAKES,
GWYNEDD

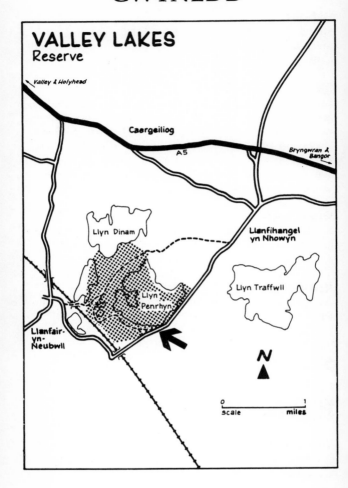

VALLEY LAKES
Reserve

Valley & Holyhead

Caergeiliog

A5

Bryngwran & Bangor

Llyn Dinam

Llanfihangel yn Nhowyn

Llyn Penrhyn

Llyn Traffwll

Llanfair-yn-Neubwll

N

0   scale   1 miles

Location

Near the north-west coast of Anglesey some two miles
(3.2 km) south-east of Valley village where the nearest
railway station is situated. SH/310770.

On the north-west coast of Anglesey, these lakes can be visited at all times via a footpath. A range of water birds can be seen throughout the year.

Habitat
The large freshwater lake of Llyn Penrhyn with several smaller reed-fringed pools and areas of fen, grassland and scrub covering 150 acres (61 ha).

Birds
Several pairs of great crested and little grebes, pochards, tufted ducks, gadwalls, shovelers and mute swans breed here with sedge and reed warblers, stonechats and reed buntings. Numerous shovelers and pochards are among the wintering wildfowl. Hen harriers and short-eared owls regularly hunt over the reserve when large finch flocks are present in winter.

Other wildlife
Locally rare plants include cyperus sedge, greater spearwort, flowering rush and marsh fen. There is a good variety of butterflies.

Visiting
The reserve may be visited at all times via public footpaths which lead from the RSPB car park at SH/315766.

Facilities
P

Warden
Alastair Moralee, Swn-y-Môr, South Stack, Holyhead, Gwynedd LL65 3HB.

i Marine Square, Salt Island Approach, Holyhead, Gwynedd LL65 1DR (tel: 0407 762622).

YNYS - HIR,

DYFED

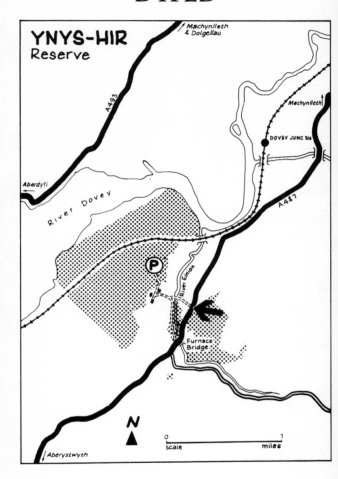

Location

Lying at the head of the Dyfi estuary, this reserve is entered from the A487 road from Machynlleth to Aberystwyth in the village of Eglwysfach. SN/686956. The nearest railway station is Dorey Junction (3 miles - 4.8 km).

Explore the beauty of Welsh oakwoods, moorland and the Dyfi Estuary. There are a number of hides overlooking the marsh and estuary. The information centre serves some refreshments.

Habitat
The grazed saltmarsh of the Dyfi Eestuary is bordered by freshwater marsh and some remnant peat bogs. Mixed deciduous and conifer woodlands, with a river gorge, rise to a rocky hillside with bracken slopes. The reserve covers 1,043 acres (422 ha).

Birds
The oakwoods contain pied flycatchers, redstarts, wood warblers, nuthatches and both great spotted and lesser spotted woodpeckers. Goldcrests and coal tits prefer the conifers and sedge and grasshopper warblers the marshland. Buzzards, kestrels and sparrowhawks breed in the woods while red-breasted mergansers and common sandpipers frequent the river. Peregrines, merlins and hen harriers hunt over the reserve outside the breeding season. Wigeons, mallards, teals and a small flock of Greenland white-fronted geese winter here.

Other wildlife
Various sundews, bog rosemary and bog asphodel grow in the bogs. Many butterfly species include dark green fritillary. Badgers and polecats occur.

Visiting
Open daily from 9 am to 9 pm or sunset when earlier. A nature trail starts from the information centre and toilets, and a number of hides are positioned by the estuary and marsh. Another is elevated in the woodland canopy.

Facilities
P £ WC IC G s ☕

Warden
Dick Squires, Cae'r Berllan, Eglwysfach, Machynlleth SY20 8TA.

i Terrace Road, Aberystwyth, Dyfed SY23 2AG (tel: 0970 612125).

Fieldfare

CASTLECALDWELL FOREST, Co FERMANAGH

CASTLECALDWELL FOREST
Reserve

Scardans Upper

Pettigoe

A 47

Leggs

Lough Scolban

Belleek

LOWER LOUGH ERNE

Rosscor

A 46

Drumbadmeen

Enniskillen

Belleek

N

0 scale 1 miles

Location

Lying on the west side of Lower Lough Erne, this peninsula is entered off the A47 road to Pettigoe four miles (6.4 km) east of Belleek. H/009603.

This reserve has pleasant trails and two hides along the shores of Lower Lough Erne. A Forest Service Information Centre, cafe and toilets are in the main car park.

Habitat
The reserve is predominantly a conifer forest fringed by bays of the lough with willow and alder scrub and reedbeds. The reserve also incorporates several islands in the lough. The reserve totals 654 acres (264 ha).

Birds
The reserve is of principal importance for common scoters which nest on the vegetated islands with mallards, tufted ducks, red-breasted mergansers, snipe and dunlins, while common and Sandwich terns use the barer ones. Sparrowhawks, long-eared owls, crossbills and siskins inhabit the forest and both great crested and little grebes the bays. Wigeons, goldeneyes, teal, pochards, tufted ducks and whooper swans occur in winter.

Other wildlife
Badger, red squirrel and pine marten inhabit the forest.

Visiting
Access at all times to the shoreline paths and two hides in Castle Bay. There is an information centre with toilets. School parties are welcome by appointment. Boat trips for small groups can be arranged with the warden.

Facilities
P   WC   IC

Warden
Joe Magee, Castlecaldwell, Leggs PO, Co Fermanagh BT93 2AG.

i Lakeland Visitor Centre, Wellington Road, Enniskillen, Co Fermanagh BT74 7EF (tel: 0365 323110).

GREEN ISLAND & GREENCASTLE POINT,

Co DOWN

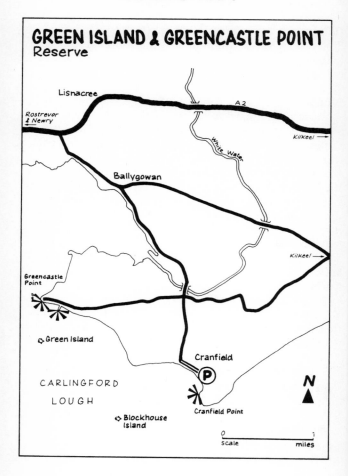

Location

A promontory in the north-east of Carlingford Lough five miles (8 km) south-west of Kilkeel. J/241118.

These small islands can be seen from a number of viewpoints on the shore. During the summer the islands are used by breeding terns and oystercatchers. There is no access to the islands.

Habitat
Both Greencastle Point and the offshore Green Island (part of the reserve) are small rocky islets covering 2 acres (0.8 ha).

Birds
The reserve has important breeding colonies of common, arctic and Sandwich terns with a few oystercatchers and ringed plovers. Small numbers of roseate terns nest in some years.

Visiting
Good views of the terns may be obtained from the coast road at Greencastle. Access to the islets is strictly prohibited to avoid disturbing the nesting birds. Black guillemots nest at the nearby Cranfield Point lighthouse.

Warden
Contact RSPB Northern Ireland Office (page 295).

i Kilkeel Leisure Centre, Kilkeel, Co Down (tel: 069 37 64666).

PORTMORE LOUGH
This new reserve is still undergoing extensive management work, but through prior arrangements with the warden limited escorted visits can be organised. It is hoped that visitor facilities will be available within the next few years. For information please contact the warden on 0846 652406 or the RSPB's Northern Ireland office 0232 491547.

LOUGH FOYLE,
Co LONDONDERRY

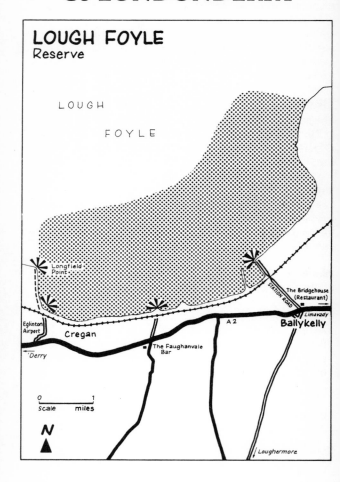

Location

The reserve embraces the south-east foreshore of Lough Foyle from Longfield Point almost to the Roe estuary. C/545237. The nearest railway station is Londonderry (8 miles - 13 km).

**Various viewpoints give excellent views over the mudflats
and adjacent fields. In early winter the Lough is an
outstanding place to see large numbers of waterfowl.**

Habitat
The reserve comprises wide mudflats covering 3,300 acres
(1,335 ha) with a fringe of saltmarsh, shingle and shell
ridges bordered by arable farmland (not within the
reserve).

Birds
Lough Foyle is outstanding for its wintering wildfowl
including thousands of wigeons, mallards, teals and pale-
bellied brent geese with oystercatchers, dunlins, bar-tailed
godwits, grey plovers and curlews. Up to 2,500 whooper
swans feed on the adjacent farmland with Bewick's swans
and white-fronted geese. Snow buntings forage on the
shore in winter when other unusual visitors include
Slavonian grebes and three species of divers. Whimbrels,
curlew sandpipers, little stints and spotted redshanks are
some of the passage migrants.

Other wildlife
Otters and common seals have been observed here.

Visiting
Access at all times to good viewpoints at Longfield Point,
Ballykelly and Faughanvale, reached by taking minor roads
off the main Limavady-Londonderry road, taking care at
the unmanned railway crossings. Visitors are asked not to
disturb the flocks of waders and wildfowl.

Warden
Contact RSPB Northern Ireland Office (page 295).

i 7 Connell street, Limavady, Co Londonderry BT49 0HA
(tel: 050 472 22226).

Bar-tailed godwit

RATHLIN ISLAND CLIFFS, Co ANTRIM

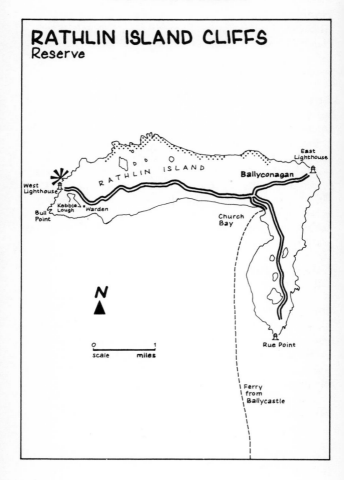

Location

The island lies five miles (8 km) across Rathlin Sound and is reached by local boat service from Ballycastle on the north Antrim coast. The nearest railway station is in Ballymoney (15 miles - 24 km).

The island is reached by ferry from Ballycastle. Visitors can then take a mini-bus to the West Light Platform. From late May to early July the platform offers spectacular views of thousands of seabirds.

Habitat
The RSPB reserve comprises 2 1/2 miles (4 km) of basalt cliffs, some high and steep, others with grassy slopes above boulder beaches. The RSPB also wardens the West Light Platform.

Birds
Large numbers of guillemots, razorbills, puffins, black guillemots, fulmars, shags, kittiwakes and both great and lesser black-backed gulls nest on the Kebble cliffs with stonechats, rock pipits and wheatears in the vicinity. Manx shearwaters nest above the northern cliffs where, as elsewhere on the island, buzzards, peregrines and ravens may be encountered. Gannets, skuas and occasionally petrels and sooty shearwaters pass offshore.

Other wildlife
Limestone bugle, thyme broomrape and several species of orchids flower on the cliffs.

Visiting
Boats leave Ballycastle most days at around 10 am. A mini-bus is available to the West Light. Please contact the warden for more information.

Warden
Contact Liam McFaul (02657) 63935; or RSPB Northern Ireland Office (page 295).

i 7 Mary Street, Ballycastle, Co Antrim BT54 6QH (tel: 02657 62024).

Mini bus
There is an irregular service across the island to Kebble.

ENQUIRIES AND COMMENTS

We welcome your comments about our nature reserves. We are continually trying to improve the habitats for wildlife and our visitors. If you have any comments or require further information on any of the nature reserves in this guide, or about the work of the RSPB in general, please contact any one of the following offices.

RSPB
The Lodge, Sandy, Bedfordshire SG19 2DL. Tel: 0767 680551

RSPB Northern Ireland Office
Belvoir Park Forest, Belfast BT8 4QT. Tel: 0232 491547

RSPB Scottish Headquarters
17 Regent Terrace, Edinburgh EH7 5BN. Tel: 031 557 3136

RSPB Wales Office
Bryn Aderyn, The Bank, Newtown, Powys SY16 2AB.
Tel: 0686 626678

RSPB East Anglia Office
Stalham House, 65 Thorpe Road, Norwich, Norfolk NR1 1UD.
Tel: 0603 660066

RSPB East Scotland Office
10 Albyn Terrace, Aberdeen AB1 1YP. Tel: 0224 624824

RSPB Central England Office
46 The Green, South Bar, Banbury, Oxfordshire OX16 9AB.
Tel: 0295 253330

RSPB North of England Office
4 Benton Terrace, Sandyford Road, Newcastle upon Tyne
NE2 1QU. Tel: 091 281 3366

RSPB North Scotland Office
Etive House, Beechwood Park, Inverness IV2 3BW.
Tel: 0463 715000

RSPB North-West England Office
Westleigh Mews, Wakefield Road, Denby Dale, Huddersfield,
West Yorkshire HD8 8QD. Tel: 0484 861148

RSPB Orkney Office
Smyril, Stenness, Stromness, Orkney KW16 3JX. Tel: 0856 850176

RSPB Shetland Office
Broonies Taing, Sandwick, Shetland ZE2 9HH. Tel: 0950 431599

RSPB South and West Scotland Office
Unit 3.1, West of Scotland Science Park, Kelvin Campus, Glasgow
G20 OSP. Tel: 041 945 5224

RSPB South-East England Office
8 Church Street, Shoreham-by-Sea, West Sussex BN43 5DQ.
Tel: 0273 463642

RSPB South-West England Office
10 Richmond Road, Exeter, Devon EX4 4JA. Tel: 0392 432691

INDEX TO RESERVES